Cats, Dogs,
and
Classroom Pets

Other Books by Barbara Dondiego
After School Crafts
Crafts for Kids: A Month-by-Month Idea Book, 2nd edition
Year-Round Crafts for Kids
Moths, Butterflies, Other Insects, and Spiders: Science in Art, Song, and Play

Cats, Dogs, and Classroom Pets

Science in Art, Song, and Play

Rhonda Vansant, Ed.D.

Barbara L. Dondiego, M.Ed.

Illustrations by

Claire Kalish

Science in Every Sense

TAB Books
Division of McGraw-Hill, Inc.
New York   San Francisco   Washington, D.C.   Auckland   Bogotá   Caracas   Lisbon   London   Madrid
Mexico City   Milan   Montreal   New Delhi   San Juan   Singapore   Sydney   Tokyo   Toronto

This book is printed on recycled paper containing a minimum of 50% total recycled fiber with 15% postconsumer de-inked fiber.

pbk   1 2 3 4 5 6 7 8 9 BBC/BBC 9 9 8 7 6 5

Product or brand names used in this book may be trade names or trademarks. Where we believe that there may be proprietary claims to such trade names or trademarks, the name has been used with an initial capital or it has been capitalized in the style used by the name claimant. Regardless of the capitalization used, all such names have been used in an editorial manner without any intent to convey endorsement of or other affiliation with the name claimant. Neither the author nor the publisher intends to express any judgment as to the validity or legal status of any such proprietary claims.

Library of Congress Cataloging-in-Publication Data
Vansant, Rhonda.
    Cats, dogs, and classroom pets : science in art, song, and play /
by Rhonda Vansant, Barbara L. Dondiego : illustrated by Claire
Kalish.
        p. cm.
    Includes index.
    ISBN 0-07-017913-1 (p)
    1. Pets—Study and teaching—Activity programs. 2. Cats—Study
and teaching—Activity programs. 3. Dogs—Study and teaching-
-Activity programs. 4. Early childhood education—Activity
programs. 5. Teaching—Aids and devices. I. Dondiego, Barbara L.
II. Kalish, Claire. III. Title.
SF416.6.V35 1995
372.3'57—dc20   94-45010
                                                                            CIP

Acquisitions editor: Kimberly Tabor
Editorial team: Jeanette R. Shearer, Book Editor
                        Joanne M. Slike, Executive Editor
                        Joann Woy, Indexer
Production team: Katherine G. Brown, Director
                        Wanda S. Ditch, Desktop Operator
                        Jeff Hall, Computer Artist
Design team: Jaclyn J. Boone, Designer   0179131
                    Kathryn Stefanski, Associate Designer   SIES

To my husband, John, for his encouragement and inspiration;
to my wonderful daughters, Melanie and Joanna,
for sharing the love of pets with me; and to Elysian,
my Old English sheepdog, my first pet,
with love.

RV

To my family for learning to cook for themselves, to iron their
own shirts, and to take care of all the pets in our home,
with love.

BD

Acknowledgments

A special thank you goes to Kim Tabor, Editor-in-Chief of TAB Books, for her guidance and encouragement throughout the conception of this series. Her advice was invaluable. We would also like to thank Jeanette Shearer, Joanne Slike, Jackie Boone, Kathryn Stefanski, Katherine Brown, Jeff Hall, Wanda Ditch, and Joann Woy of TAB/McGraw-Hill for all their hard work and dedication.

Contents

A Letter to Teachers

Dear Teachers,

You might be one of many educators who feels a certain anxiety about teaching science. Perhaps your science courses in school and college were stressful as you plodded through specific experiments, tried to memorize the periodic table, and tried to understand phenomena without the opportunity to build concepts first. You probably have forgotten much of the science instruction because much of it went only in short-term memory and had no direct link to what you were encountering in your world at that time. Perhaps you never had a role model who felt a passion about loving and caring for the world—a role model who would dare to teach you "how" to learn rather than "what" to learn.

Whether you place yourself in this category or were blessed with good role models who instilled in you a zeal for learning science, we hope this book will contribute to meaningful and enjoyable science instruction in your class.

Because we embrace the definition that science for young children is studying and exploring our world, we strongly feel that science should be the focus of an Early Childhood curriculum. Although this is a science book, it is also a book about life and learning. It is designed to serve as a framework for a thematic study. We have provided many teaching and learning activities that involve varied content areas. Within this framework, you can also creatively add your own literature, math experiences, writing experiences, and other activities that meet the specific needs of your children. The format of this book allows your teaching and learning experiences to flow naturally together in an integrated way.

The time that it takes to complete the various activities depends on the age of the children and the number of children involved. The time involved is also affected by the ways you integrate the learning activities in this book with other aspects of the curriculum.

We hope that you will find this to be a comfortable format for teaching science and that you will enjoy, with your students, the journey of discovery. Perhaps you will be one who inspires this generation of children to find joy and excitement in learning about the wonders that surround us.

Sincerely,

Rhonda Vansant

A Letter to Parents

Dear Parents,

Generations of children have grown up feeling that science was too difficult, too stressful. Many children have avoided science and ranked it among their least favorite subjects.

How wonderful to think that we might change that attitude for the current generation. We the authors view science as studying and exploring our world in ways that are appropriate for the learner's stage of development. Children explore the world quite naturally, and we want to build upon the natural inclinations of children by guiding their explorations and nurturing their curiosity. When children see their ice cream melt, they have an opportunity to learn about their world. When children feel the wind blow, they are discovering information about their world. We do not have to search for expensive equipment to teach science to young children; we simply need to take advantage of everything that is already around us.

One of the most precious gifts we can give our children is a love of learning. We hope you will find ways to use this book with your own children as well as with groups of children in various organizations. It is our hope that you will nurture your children's natural wonder and curiosity about our world and that the dream that this generation will come to love, understand, and cherish this world will come true.

Sincerely,

Rhonda Vansant

Introduction

Pets are ideal science subjects for young children because most children have a pet, have seen someone's pet, or have a pet in their classroom. As children learn that pets need loving care and give us companionship and enjoyment, they develop a respect for living things. Studying pets also fosters children's natural curiosity about the world around them and encourages them to use their five senses.

Building concepts

Pets allow children to study a real object or living thing. This is called a *concrete experience*. If the topic of study is fish, for example, we should provide children with opportunities to see and investigate real fish. When we do so, we are *building a concept*. Concepts are the foundation for subsequent learning. After children experience reality, they can then make models or re-create the experience in a variety of ways. Models and pictures are called *semi-concrete representations*. Words that we attach to these experiences are called *symbolic representations*. The word *cat* written in a book symbolizes a living and breathing animal that we experience many times in our lives. Giving children opportunities to experience real living and nonliving things helps them develop concepts that, in turn, give meaning to the written and spoken word.

Cats, Dogs, and Other Classroom Pets provides opportunities for children to build concepts by introducing them to a variety of household pets beginning with cats and dogs, and including mice, gerbils, hamsters, rabbits, guinea pigs, fish, and birds. It is written as a cross-curricular guide to enable parents and teachers to teach children about pets all day long if desired! Each animal study includes some or all of the following:

☐ **Art** Creating artistic or lifelike models of the animal

☐ **Creative drama** Dressing up and pretending to be an animal

☐ **Music and dancing** Singing songs and moving creatively to express ideas and feelings about the animal

☐ **Literature** Listening to animal stories

☐ **Research** Using the five senses to find out about an animal, finding pictures of them, talking to people about animals, and writing reports about animals

☐ **Creative writing** Writing (or telling) stories and poems

☐ **Cooking** Creating animal treats such as carrot sticks, apple wedges, and homemade dog biscuits

☐ **Mathematics** Learning cooking activities and creating models used to teach math concepts such as making a bar graph, studying standard measure using a ruler and a tape measure, making geometric shapes, using a watch to tell time, working with fractions, and working with solid and liquid measures

The book provides factual information to be read aloud to children. You might want to sit in a comfortable chair and have the children sit on the floor in front of you. If you keep a chart of important words for the children's future writing, place it nearby so that you can add words throughout your reading and discussion time. Your chart might look like this as you add words of interest to the children:

Cats	
fur	paws
ears	meow
nose	tail

or

Parts of a Cat I Can See:	How a Cat Feels:	Sounds a Cat Makes:	Things Cats Like To Do:
ears	soft	meow	play
eyes	fluffy	hiss	sleep
tail	furry	purr	lick
		growl	eat

Teaching children science

For young children, science should not be a set of experiments with specific steps that must be followed. It should involve a very natural discovery of their world through real experiences, creative art, literature, drama, music, writing, reading, and play. Whenever we teach children to use their five senses, we are teaching science. Whenever we provide opportunities for exploration and discovery, we are teaching science. Whenever we help children get to know the world around them, we are teaching science. Whenever we teach children to love and care for the world, we are teaching science.

The following science skills are appropriate for instruction with young children. You will be helping children use these skills as you pursue your study of pets.

1. *Observing* Using any of the five senses to become aware of objects
2. *Classifying* Arranging objects or information in groups according to some method
3. *Creating models* Portraying information through multisensory representations
4. *Manipulating materials* Handling materials safely and effectively
5. *Measuring* Making quantitative observations (time, temperature, weight, length, etc.)

6. *Using numbers* Applying mathematical rules
7. *Asking questions* Verbally demonstrating curiosity
8. *Finding information* Locating words, pictures, or numbers
9. *Making predictions* Suggesting what might happen (Predictions should come after children have some experiences with the topic. Predictions should be based on previously gathered data.)
10. *Designing investigations* Coming up with a plan to find out information or answers to questions
11. *Communicating or recording information* Communicating or recording by the following:
    - talking to the teacher and/or other children
    - playing with theme-related props
    - drawing pictures
    - labeling
    - making diagrams
    - making graphs
    - writing (descriptive in learning logs or narrative)
    - making photographs with a camera
    - recording on audio or videotape
12. *Drawing conclusions* Coming to various conclusions based on their stage of cognitive growth and their prior experiences
13. *Applying knowledge* Finding ways to use what is learned

About this book

Each chapter starts with a science goal to guide the parents and teachers. The goal is followed by ideas on how to plan for the activities, as well as lists of visual aids and related words that can be used for discussion.

Safety symbols, or icons, have been placed in the text to alert parents and teachers about activities that require supervision or other precautions.

 Scissors

 Adult supervision

Discussion Ideas, Activity Ideas, and Science Skills are also indicated by symbols in the text:

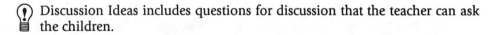 Discussion Ideas includes questions for discussion that the teacher can ask the children.

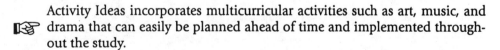 Activity Ideas incorporates multicurricular activities such as art, music, and drama that can easily be planned ahead of time and implemented throughout the study.

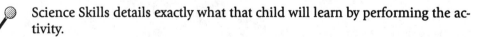 Science Skills details exactly what that child will learn by performing the activity.

Pet Pause and Let's Create are interspersed throughout the text. Pet Pause contains useful tidbits of information intended to be passed along verbally to the children or instructional information for the teacher or parent. Let's

Create includes directions and simple patterns so the children can build actual models of the animals being studied. Children personify objects quite naturally; they enjoy giving their models names and personalities as they use them in a variety of ways. They can create animal ears and noses to wear so they can pretend to be the animal. Sometimes they make toys for the animal. All of the Let's Create ideas can be embellished with a child's creative thoughts of how an animal might look or behave. The models can then be used in pre-planned activities as well as in spontaneous play.

A final word

For parents and teachers, every moment is an opportunity to teach science. By using this book, children will experience real animals, create models of animals, hear and read stories about them, act out animal plays, sing animal songs, and truly come to know animals in many ways. As each child moves from the real to the semi-concrete to the symbolic, he or she gains a true understanding of pets in the world. We hope the children enjoy studying pets by performing the activities in this book. More importantly, we hope that their sensitivity to the living creatures in their world will be enhanced.

CATS

Science goals

To help children become aware of what cats are like, how they behave as pets, and how we can take care of them

Teacher/Parent planning

Think about how you can get a real cat to the class for a visit. You might try to ask a parent volunteer to bring a cat in by sending a note home a week before you start your study. Contact a local veterinarian about visiting the classroom. Borrow books from the library. Prepare to write words about cats on a large sheet of chart paper. Ask children to bring in pictures of their cats.

Materials needed for discussion and activities

- ☐ A live kitten or cat
- ☐ Toy cats (stuffed animals)
- ☐ Informational books from the library
- ☐ Storybooks from the library
- ☐ Newspapers (classified section)
- ☐ Magazines
- ☐ Paints and brushes
- ☐ Tape recorder
- ☐ "The Three Little Kittens" rhyme
- ☐ *Lady and the Tramp* video

Related words

mammal An animal that has a backbone, hair or fur, is warm-blooded, and whose young are born alive and drink milk from their mother

iris The colored part of the eye that surrounds the pupil or black part

paw The foot of a four-legged animal that also has claws

claw A sharp, curved nail on the paw of an animal

veterinarian A person trained to give medical care to animals

> **Pet pause** *Throughout this unit of study, let your children keep "learning logs." These logs are journals where young scientists write down their science data.*

Cats

A cat can be a loving, playful, entertaining pet. Many people get a kitten so that they can enjoy watching it grow up and play. Other people get a grown cat who needs a new home. You can get a kitten or grown cat from a pet store, an animal shelter in your city, a friend, or a relative, or sometimes by answering an advertisement in the newspaper. Sometimes a cat becomes your pet by finding you. Stray cats wander around in search of someone to keep them and take care of them. If you adopt a stray, make certain to have it checked out by a veterinarian.

Visiting with a cat

 ### *Observing*

"Today we have a special visitor. _____ has brought his (or her) kitten to share with us. He (or she) will hold the kitten while we quietly watch and listen as he (or she) tells us about the kitten. Then we can watch the kitten as it plays in the cat carrier." Encourage the visitor to share for about 15 minutes, then allow time for the children to ask questions.

"If you have a cat for a pet, where did you get your cat? How did you decide on getting it? How old was it when you got it?"

Locating information in the newspaper

 ### *Finding information*

Help children look through the newspaper to find ads for kittens or grown cats to be given away or for sale.

A cat's ears are at the top of its head and are shaped like triangles. A cat's nose is small and shaped like a triangle. The colored part of a cat's eyes, called the iris, can be green, yellow, orange, blue, or lavender. The black part, called the pupil, changes size because it controls how much light can come into the cat's eyes. Whiskers are special hairs that grow near the cat's mouth and above its eyes. They are sensitive touch organs that send messages to the cat's brain about objects the whiskers touch.

Looking at a cat

Observing; recording information; manipulating materials; asking questions; making predictions

Help children look at the parts of the head and face of the cat you are observing. Encourage children to be gentle and quiet as they observe the cat. Let children pet the cat if the owner thinks the cat will not mind, but take extra precautions about safety. You don't want anyone to get scratched or bitten. Remind children that cats do not like sudden noises or being grabbed. Encourage the children to ask questions. Let the children make predictions about what might happen if the cat gets frightened.

At the easel in the art center, let children paint cat faces. They will enjoy using the colors of eyes mentioned in the text and painting on the whiskers.

When a kitten is born, it is so small that it can fit in one of your hands. Kittens need to stay with their mother for about two months before they find a new home. They continue to grow and grow. Cats are usually 8 to 10 inches tall, but can be taller or shorter. Cats weigh about 7 to 15 pounds when they are fully grown.

Cats are mammals, which means they have hair, are warm-blooded, feed milk to their kittens, and breathe with lungs. Hair protects their skin and keeps them warm. Cats can be black, gray or bluish, brown, white, and various shades of red, yellow, or orange. Cats can have stripes or patches of color. Cats have short hair or long hair.

💡 *What a cat looks like*

🔍 *Communicating information*
"If you have a cat, tell us what it looks like." If the children have brought pictures of their cats, let them show their pictures and introduce their cats to the class.

☞ *Making a "cat-alog"*

🔍 *Categorizing; recording information*
Start a "cat-alog" of photographs, magazine pictures or pictures of cats drawn by the children. The "cat-alog" will be a fun book to create. Children might want to categorize the cats in some way, according to the type, color, size, name, and so on.

Let's Create a Tabletop Cat and Kitten

🔍 *Using a ruler to measure inches; learning about rectangles; manipulating materials; following directions; learning about the anatomy of an animal by creating a model; using reference material; recording information*

The Tabletop Cat and Kitten
The tabletop cat got its name because its back is flat like a table and it has four legs (Fig. 1-1). If you write a short report about cats, it can be glued to the cat's back. The kitten is easy to make from an unlined index card.

■ 1-1 *The Tabletop Cat and Kitten.*

What you need

- White poster board
- 3-x-5-inch unlined index cards
- Construction paper
- Ruler
- Pencil
- Scissors
- White glue
- Markers
- Crayons

Directions to make the Tabletop Cat

1. Use the ruler and pencil to draw a 5-x-10-inch rectangle on white poster board. Cut the rectangle out. The diagram (Fig. 1-2) shows you how to measure, cut, and fold the rectangle to make the body and legs of the cat. Remember to make it look like a table.

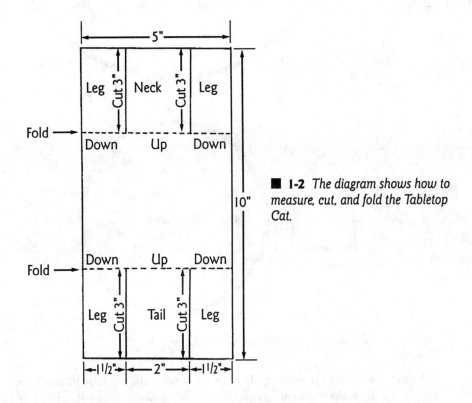

■ **1-2** *The diagram shows how to measure, cut, and fold the Tabletop Cat.*

2. Bend the four legs down. Bend the neck and tail up. Cut the corners off the tail and then fringe it so it looks fluffy.
3. Use the patterns (Fig. 1-3) to trace and cut out the circle cat head and the cat ears from construction paper. Color the cat head. Add eyes, nose, mouth, and whiskers. Glue the ears to the head.

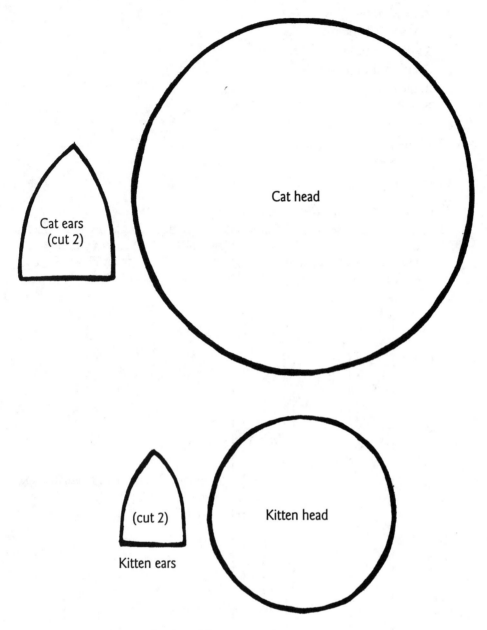

■ **I-3** *The patterns for the Tabletop Cat and Kittens.*

4. Color the cat's entire body. Draw some claws. Glue the head onto the neck. To make the head stand up straight, measure and cut a 1-×-3-inch rectangle from construction paper. Fold it into the letter *Z*. Glue the top of the *Z* to the back of the cat's neck. Glue the bottom of the *Z* to the back of the cat (Fig. 1-4).

Directions to make the Tabletop Kitten

 1. Use the pattern (Fig. 1-5) to cut and fold the 3-×-5-inch index card. Fold the legs down to make the card look like a table. Fold the neck and tail up. Trim the tail and fringe it.

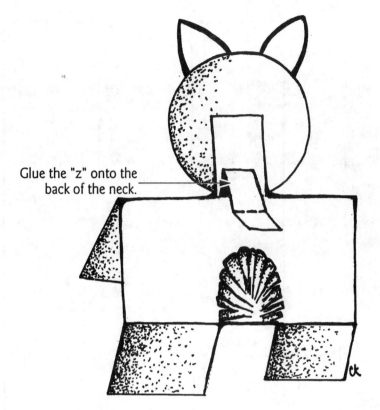

Glue the "z" onto the
back of the neck.

■ **1-4** *The back of the Tabletop Cat.*

2. Use the patterns in Fig. 1-3 to trace and cut out the kitten head and ears from construction paper. Color the head and draw on a cat face. Glue the ears to the head. Color the entire kitten. Glue the head to the neck. By using more index cards you can make as many kittens as you want.

For Pre-K through First Grade Help the children find and select stories of real and imaginary cats that you can read to them. Use a large piece of paper such as a chart tablet or a big book to record a class story about a real cat, dictated to you by the children. Help them record a second story about an imaginary cat. If they wish to, they can write cat vocabulary words on the back of their tabletop cats and kittens.

For Grades Two and Three Help the children find interesting books about all kinds of cats. Each child can choose a cat to learn about and to share with the class. The children can write a class story or a class play to be acted out by their tabletop cats and kittens. Interesting spelling and vocabulary words that they encounter can be written on cards and glued on the back of the tabletop cat.

Cats have five toes on each front paw, including one special toe that looks kind of like a thumb. They have four toes on each back paw. Some cats even have extra toes.

Each toe has a sharp claw. Cats use the claws to climb, to catch other animals, to help them grab onto things, and to defend themselves. Cats can move very

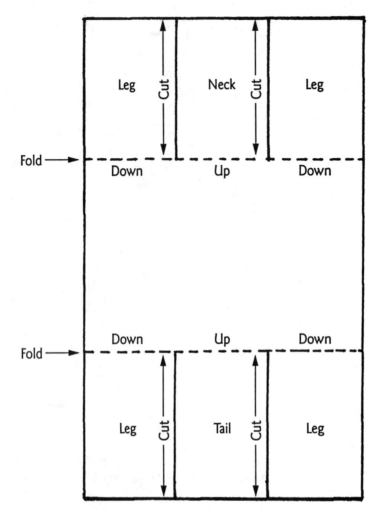

■ **I-5** *The pattern for the Tabletop Kitten.*

quietly because the bottom of a cat's feet are like soft pillows. These soft pillows are called pads.

Cats "talk" to us and each other by making many kinds of sounds. "Meow" can mean hello or it can mean that the cat is curious, hungry, or lonely. "Purring" can mean that your cat is happy. "Hisses," "growls," and "screams" might mean your cat is angry or afraid.

A cat might tell you it wants to play by rolling over and waving its paw. It might tell you it is angry or afraid by waving its tail back and forth, arching its back, or puffing up its fur.

 Sharing cat experiences

 Communicating information
"If you have a cat, tell us about a time when your cat made sounds or did something that gave you a message."

☞ *Record or dictate*

🔍 *Communicating information*

Tape-record these stories, let children dictate them to you, or let them write them. Let children illustrate their stories.

Kittens are very playful. They like to run and chase things. They sometimes jump out at your feet as you walk by. You can buy special toys made for kittens or make some of your own. An old sock makes a good toy for a kitten. Be careful not to give your cat string or yarn because it could get wrapped around its neck. Kittens like to watch everything that is going on. They are very active but also take long naps. When cats are grown, they play less and sleep more.

☞ *Singing and acting*

🔍 *Applying knowledge; communicating information*

Use the song "Cats Walk Softly." It is an echo song in which the teacher sings (or says) each line and the children repeat it. Children should act out each line as it is sung. The song ends very quietly because the cats are asleep.

Cats Walk Softly

Composed by Rhonda Vansant
Arranged by Elizabeth Dondiego

Cats walk soft-ly. (echo)

Cats say me-ow. (echo)

Cats like to run and play (echo)

But it's time to sleep now. (echo)

To stay healthy, a cat needs regular visits to the veterinarian. The veterinarian will talk to you about taking care of your cat and will give it medicines to keep it from getting certain diseases.

☞ *Setting up a cat clinic*

Classifying; manipulating materials; measuring; using numbers; communicating and recording information; applying knowledge
Let children set up a "cat clinic" in the dramatic play area. Children can bring toy cats from home to be the patients. Provide a telephone, appointment book, files, bandages, empty containers for pretend medicine, and any other materials for pretend play.

Cats clean themselves. They lick their fur with their tongue. They rub their fur with their paws. You should brush or comb your cat each day.

Let's Create Mother Cat Ears, Kitten Ears, and Cat Noses

Manipulating materials; following directions; creating models; learning about cats by imitating their actions.
Create and wear the mother cat ears, kitten ears, and cat noses when acting out "The Three Little Kittens" and when singing and dancing to the song "Cats Walk Softly." You might write your own cat story and wear the ears and noses to act it out.

What you need
- ☐ Two paper plates (The white cheap plates are best.)
- ☐ White poster board
- ☐ Scissors
- ☐ Stapler
- ☐ Crayons
- ☐ Construction paper
- ☐ Two large hairpins or string to tie on the ears
- ☐ String to tie on the nose

Directions to make the Kitten Ears

1. To make the kitten ears (Fig. 1-6), begin by folding a paper plate in half. Press it with your fingers on the fold to make it flat. Cut out the half-circle middle of the plate to form a headband (Fig. 1-7).
2. Use the kitten ear pattern (Fig. 1-8) to cut two ears from the leftover plate middle. Color each ear. Then cut a slit in each, as shown on the pattern. Overlap the bottom and staple it (Fig. 1-9).
3. Color the headband. Insert the ears in the top. Staple the headband two times at the base of each ear (Fig. 1-6).
4. Fasten the headband on your head with two large hairpins or with string tied through the ends.

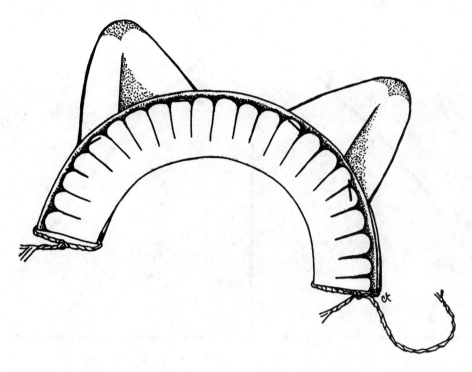

■ **1-6** *The Cat Ears.*

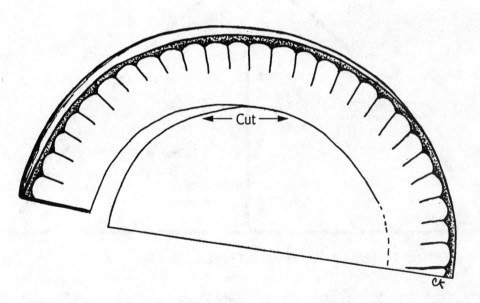

■ **1-7** *Fold the plate in half. Cut out the middle.*

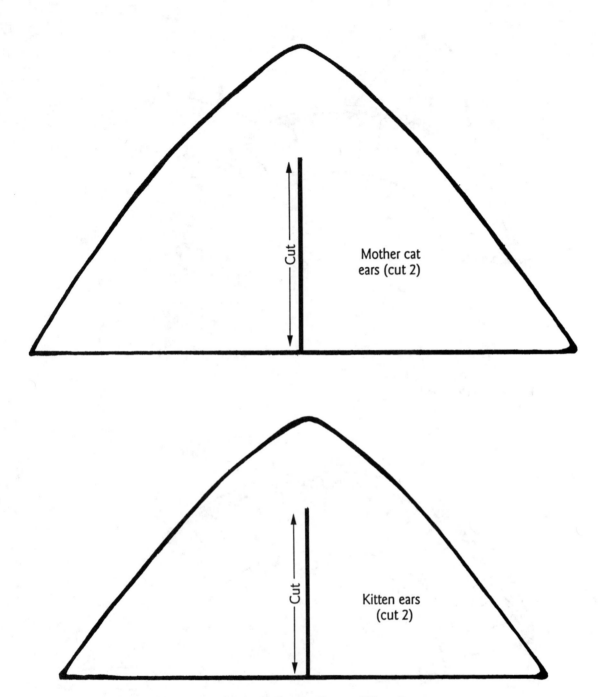

Cut

Mother cat
ears (cut 2)

Cut

Kitten ears
(cut 2)

■ **I-8** *The patterns for the Mother Cat Ears and Kitten Ears.*

Directions to make the Mother Cat Ears

Follow the directions above to make the headband. Trace the mother cat ear pattern (Fig. 1-8) onto poster board. Follow the remaining directions above to complete the ears.

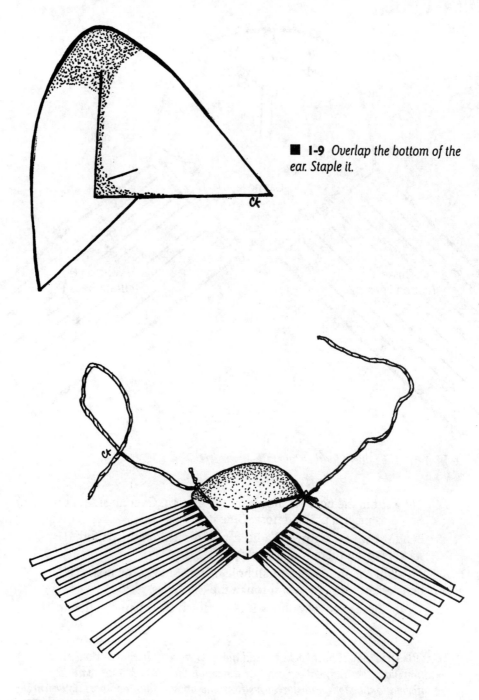

■ **1-9** *Overlap the bottom of the ear. Staple it.*

■ **1-10** *The Cat Nose.*

Directions to make the Cat Nose

1. To make the cat nose (Fig. 1-10), trace the nose pattern (Fig. 1-11) onto poster board. Cut the pattern out. Color the nose pink and the whiskers black or brown.

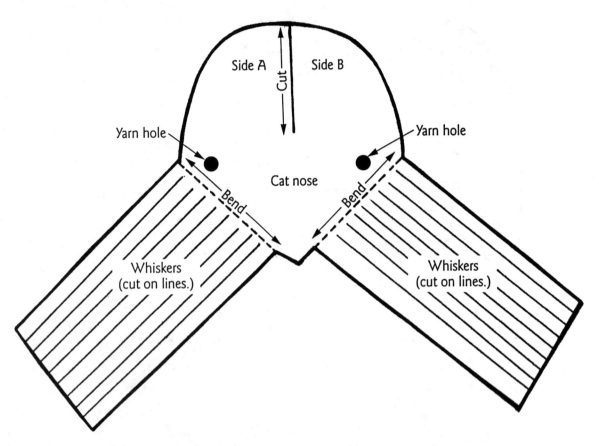

■ **I-II** *The pattern for the Cat Nose.*

2. Cut a slit in the nose, as shown on the pattern. Overlap side A on top of side B to make a pointed nose. Glue it.

3. Bend the whiskers forward a little, as indicated on the pattern. Use scissors to cut them into thin strips.

 4. An adult should make a small hole in each side of the nose. Tie lightweight string or yarn through the two holes.

5. Tie the nose over your nose with the cat whiskers hanging down.

> ***Pet pause*** *Select books to read aloud to the children at various times throughout the study. Allow time for the children to look at and read the informational books and storybooks from the library. Plan appropriate writing experiences for the children. A thematic chart of words about cats will be helpful to children as they write.*

 Acting

Applying knowledge
Let the children have fun acting out "The Three Little Kittens," which is a familiar rhyme about cleanliness. The teacher can read the rhyme and let the

children act it out in their own creative ways or the children can read or say their own lines while they act out their parts.

What you need

☐ Three pairs of kitten ears
☐ One pair of mother cat ears
☐ Four cat noses
☐ Three pairs of mittens (optional)
☐ Clothesline on which to hang the mittens (optional)

Cats can learn to respond to their name. They can learn what "no" means when they misbehave. They need lots of praise and petting for good behavior. The more often you talk to them, the more words they will understand.

☞ Talking about animated cats

Finding information

Show portions of the movie *Lady and the Tramp* in which the Siamese cats are causing problems. Lead the children in a discussion of the behavior of the cats.

Cats scratch at objects. Scratching helps to take off worn parts of their claws. A scratching post covered with carpet is a good thing for cats to scratch on.

Cats who live indoors should have a litter box. The litter box should be filled with cat litter you buy, shredded newspaper, or sand.

Cats like cozy, warm places to rest and sleep. A box with a blanket makes a good bed for a cat. Cats often like to sleep on window sills where they can enjoy warm sunshine. If your cat lives indoors, it might like to sleep on your bed or even sleep with you at night.

☞ Creating cat beds

Creating models; applying knowledge

Ask children to bring stuffed toy cats, old boxes, and soft blankets to make cozy beds for the cats. The children might enjoy decorating the boxes with pictures they can glue on or with their own drawings.

Cats like quiet, calm activities. Some cats like to be held while they sleep. They like for you to talk to them in a calm voice and pet them or gently scratch their head. Some cats like you to read to them. Have you ever thought about reading to your cat?

☞ Reading to our cats

Communicating information

Let children read stories about cats to their toy cats during your quiet reading time.

Give your cat plenty of attention and love and, hopefully, it will have a long life. Most healthy cats live about 12 to 15 years.

Finding cats in books

Finding information

Go to the library to get books about cats. Check out the C encyclopedia also and let children find the section on cats. Let the children sit on the floor with their books. Call out each item and let the children try to find it in their books and share it with the class after you call on them.

See if you can find a cat with

1. Gray hair
2. Two different colors of hair
3. Short hair
4. Long hair
5. Blue eyes
6. Yellow eyes

Point to

1. Whiskers
2. Ears
3. Eyes
4. Nose
5. Tail

Older children who are reading well can select a certain type of cat to write a report on or write a story about it. The report should be brief and can be glued to the back or stomach of the tabletop cat. If more pages are needed, the cat could become a book if the pages are stapled to its back.

 Closure

Communicating information; drawing conclusions; applying knowledge; designing investigations

Bringing closure to your study is important. Review the initial goals and give children opportunities to talk about what they have learned. Let them share their favorite parts of the study. Help them talk about ways they can use what they have learned. If children want to design further investigations, help them do so.

chapter 2

DOGS

Science goals

To help children become aware of what dogs are like, how they behave as pets, and how we can take care of them

Teacher/Parent planning

Think about how you can get a real dog to the class for a visit. A puppy (or puppies) can be more enjoyable and safer than a grown dog. You might want to acquire parent volunteers to bring dogs by sending a note home a week before you start your study. Your local animal shelter might be willing to visit and bring puppies. If you want a veterinarian to visit, go ahead and contact one. Borrow books from the library. Prepare to write words about dogs on a large sheet of chart paper. Ask children to bring in pictures of their dogs.

Materials needed for discussion and activities

- ☐ One or more live puppies or grown dogs
- ☐ Toy dogs
- ☐ Informational books from the library
- ☐ Newspaper (classified section)
- ☐ Magazines
- ☐ Paints and brushes

Related words

mammal An animal that has hair or fur, is warm-blooded, whose young are born alive and drink milk from their mother, and breathes with lungs

paw The foot of a four-legged animal that also has claws

veterinarian A person trained to give medical care to animals

> **Pet pause** *Remember that children need to experience real objects or living things before they encounter symbolic representations.*

Dogs

Dogs can be helpful, playful, loving, and obedient pets. Many people choose to get a puppy so they can enjoy watching it grow up, play, and learn to carry out specific tasks through training. Some people get a grown dog who needs a new home. You can get a puppy or grown dog from a pet store, an animal shelter in your city, a friend or relative, or by answering an advertisement in the newspaper. A dog can become your pet by it finding you. Dogs who have no home sometimes wander around in search of someone to love them and take care of them. If you adopt a stray, be sure to have it checked out by a veterinarian.

 Visiting with a dog

 Observing

"Today we have a special visitor." The visitor should share information about the dog and allow children to pet the dog if that is safe and appropriate. Ask the owner to tell the children how much the dog weighs and how tall it is in inches. Any measuring or weighing while the dog is there would be beneficial. Have a ruler and tape measure on hand to measure the length of its tail, ears, legs, and so on. Encourage the visitor to share for about 15 minutes, then allow time for the children to ask questions.

"If you have a dog for a pet, where did you get your dog? How did you decide to get it? How old was it when you got it?"

☞ *Locating information in the newspaper*

Finding information
Help children look through the newspaper to find ads for dogs to be given away or for sale.

Let's Create a Paper Plate Dog

Observing and re-creating an animal; manipulating materials; following directions
One pattern is used to create two ears, two back feet, and two front paws. A paper plate becomes the dog's head. It's easy to invent your favorite paper plate dog (Fig. 2-1). When your dog is finished, tape a paint stick on the back to turn it into a puppet. Enter it in a dog show!

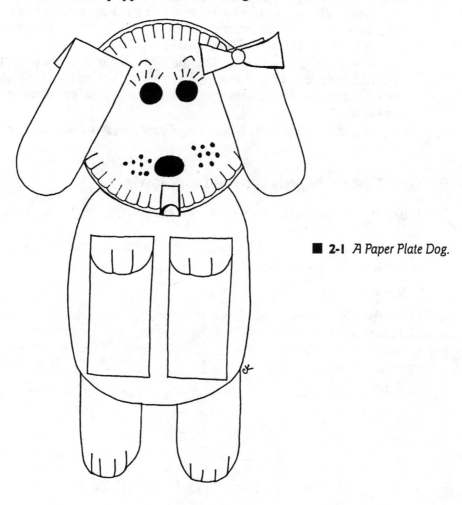

■ **2-1** *A Paper Plate Dog.*

What you need
- ☐ Construction paper, including black and red
- ☐ Scissors
- ☐ 9-inch white paper plate
- ☐ Stapler
- ☐ Markers
- ☐ Crayons
- ☐ White glue
- ☐ Paint stirring stick from a hardware store
- ☐ Masking tape or packing tape

Directions

1. To make the body of the dog, use scissors to trim the corners of a 9-x-12-inch piece of construction paper. The color of the paper you should use depends on the color of the dog you want to make. For example, use white paper if you want to create a dalmatian and add black spots. Use brown paper to make a beagle; use black paper to make a Labrador retriever.

2. To make the head, staple or glue the paper plate onto the body. Color the head and body with crayons to make it look like your favorite dog.

3. Use the patterns (Fig. 2-2) to trace and cut out six ear/paw shapes, a tail, two black circle eyes, a black oval nose, and a red tongue. Look at the fold lines on the ear/paw pattern. Fold two of the shapes to make ears, two to make front paws, and two to make back feet.

4. Use glue to assemble your dog. Glue the tail on the back of the body. If you want, you can design a bow for the dog's ear, a bone for its mouth, or a collar for its neck. Use markers to add whisker dots, eyelashes, and paw marks.

5. Tape a paint stirring stick on the back of your dog so he can join the dog show.

Let's Create Awards for the Dog Show

Learning to categorize; using reference material; recording data; using descriptive terms

Design and decorate prizes for the entrants in the show. Be creative and add ribbons, glitter, and other fancy things.

What you need
- ☐ Construction paper
- ☐ Markers
- ☐ Scissors
- ☐ Glue
- ☐ Tape

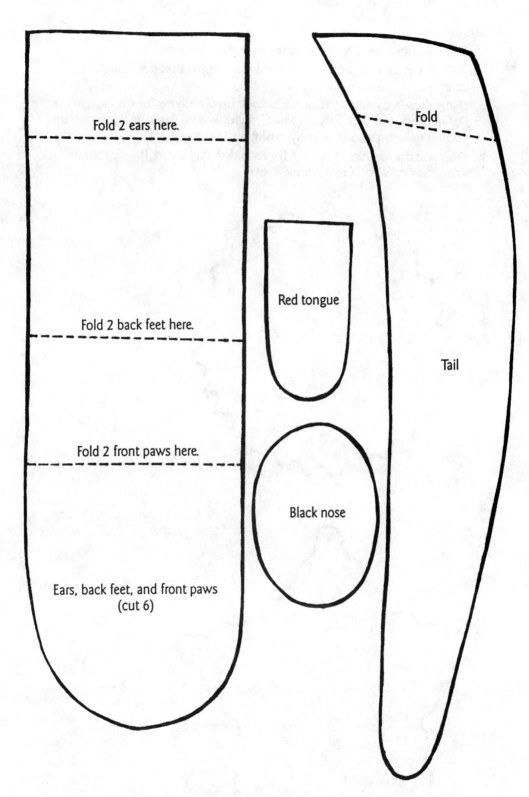

Fold 2 ears here.

Fold

Red tongue

Tail

Fold 2 back feet here.

Fold 2 front paws here.

Black nose

Ears, back feet, and front paws
(cut 6)

■ **2-2** *The patterns for the Paper Plate Dog.*

Directions

1. Use the patterns in Fig. 2-3 to trace and cut out awards.
2. Write the prize category on the award. Add words that describe that category.
3. Use a dictionary and a thesaurus to look up synonyms for the category. For instance, if a dog wins the Most Playful award, describe the award by adding synonyms such as lively, frisky, and frolicsome.
4. Decorate the awards. Make one for each dog that enters the dog show. Tape the awards on the winning dogs.

■ **2-3** *The patterns for the Dog Show Awards.*

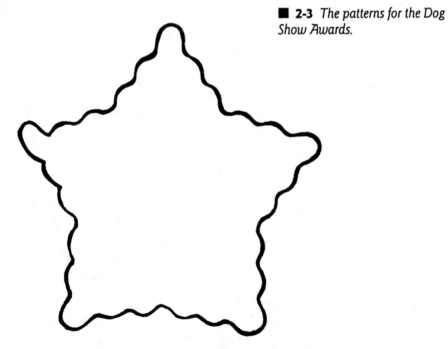

Dogs are mammals, which means that they have hair, are warm-blooded, feed milk to their puppies, and breathe with lungs. A mother can give birth to 1 or maybe even 15 puppies. When puppies are born, their eyes are closed and their ears are closed. During the first few weeks of their lives, they stay very close to their mother. They need to stay with their mother for about six to eight weeks before they have a new home.

Pet pause *Why do dogs pant? Dogs' bodies do not cool off by sweating. A dog cools its body by sticking out its tongue and panting. Evaporation of water from the dog's mouth cools its body.*

Let's Create a Paper Plate Puppy

Observing and re-creating an animal baby; manipulating materials; following directions

This playful puppy costs less than a penny to make because it's designed from a cheap paper plate (Fig. 2-4).

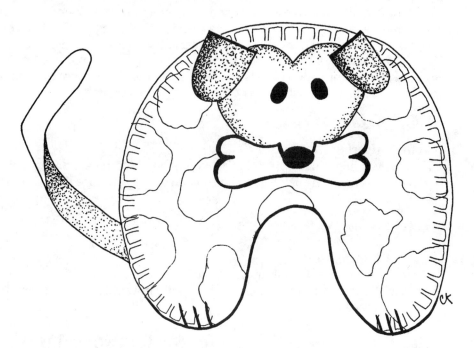

■ **2-4** *A Paper Plate Puppy.*

What you need

- ☐ 9-inch white paper plate
- ☐ Scissors
- ☐ Markers or crayons
- ☐ Construction paper
- ☐ White glue

Directions

1. Use the bell pattern (Fig. 2-5) to cut the legs of the paper plate puppy. To do this, first trace the pattern and cut it out. Then lay the pattern on the plate so the bottom of the bell is even with the plate edge. Trace around the pattern. Cut the bell shape out of the plate.

2. Use markers or crayons to color the body of the puppy.

3. Trace the patterns in Fig. 2-5. From construction paper, cut out a head, tail, nose, two ears, two eyes, and a bone. Follow the directions of the patterns to fold the ears and to cut a snout on the head.

4. Glue the head near the top of the body. Add ears and eyes. Glue the nose on the end of the snout. Glue the bone in the puppy's mouth. Glue the tail on the back of the body so that it shows in front.

There are hundreds of kinds of dogs throughout the world. Some dogs grow up to be very big and some are very small. Dogs come in many colors. They can be many shades of brown, black, gray, bluish, and white. They can be shades of red, yellow, or orange. They might have spots. They might have long hair or short hair. Dogs have long tails or short tails.

A purebred dog is one whose father and mother are the same kind of dog. If the mother is a collie and the father is a collie, then the puppies will be collies. Some examples of these kinds of dogs are golden retriever, cocker spaniel, Great Dane, terrier, dalmatian, and poodle. Some dogs are mixed-breeds. For instance, if the mother is a collie and the father is a golden retriever, the puppies will be a mixed-breed. These dogs turn out to be very unique.

 What a dog looks like

 Communicating information
"If you have a dog, tell us what it looks like." If the children have brought pictures of their dogs, let them show their pictures and introduce their dogs to the class.

 Looking at various breeds

 Finding information
Allow children time to look in the encyclopedia and other informational books at the many breeds of dogs. Children might want to choose a certain type of dog to do a report about.

Let's Create Junk Mail Dogs for Grades Two and Up

 Learning to measure; using reference material; categorizing; creating models; learning the sizes, shapes, and anatomy of different breeds of dogs; manipulating materials; following directions
Although cats look basically the same, dogs come in all sorts of shapes and sizes. Junk mail (mail that nobody in the house wants to read) comes in all sorts of shapes and sizes, too. When the junk mail arrives, ask your parents if you can have it. Open the envelopes carefully, and use them to create and stuff all kinds of dogs!

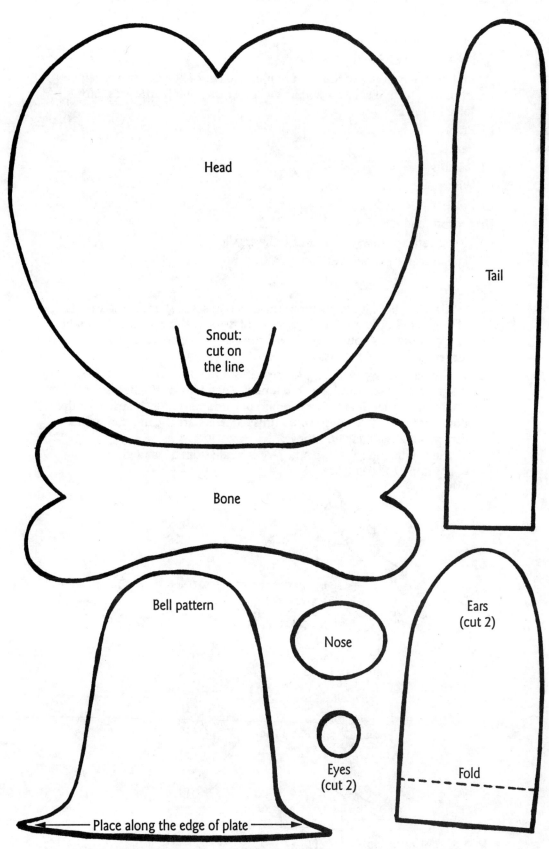

Head

Tail

Snout:
cut on
the line

Bone

Bell pattern

Nose

Ears
(cut 2)

Eyes
(cut 2)

Fold

Place along the edge of plate

■ **2-5** *The patterns for the Paper Plate Puppy.*

What you need

☐ Books about different breeds of dogs
☐ Junk mail envelopes of different shapes and sizes (You can use envelopes from long business letters, square greeting cards, small gift cards, plus large brown envelopes.)
☐ Ruler
☐ Pencil
☐ Scissors
☐ White glue
☐ Poster board
☐ Crayons and markers
☐ Tissue paper or newspaper to stuff the envelopes
☐ Tape to seal the envelopes

Directions

1. Use the dog book to learn about the different sizes, shapes, and breeds of dogs. Find out about the categories of dogs. For instance, dogs might be categorized as hound breeds, sporting dogs, nonsporting breeds, terriers, working dogs, and toy breeds.

2. To decide what types of dogs to create from the junk mail envelopes, first measure each envelope with a ruler. Then trace the patterns for the dogs onto poster board. Poster board or cardboard must be used for the dogs' legs so they stand up when finished. Here are the measurements for five junk mail dog envelopes:
   • The chihuahua (Figs. 2-6 and 2-7) is made from a small gift card envelope 2 × 2½ inches.

■ **2-6** *The Chihuahua Junk Mail Dog.*

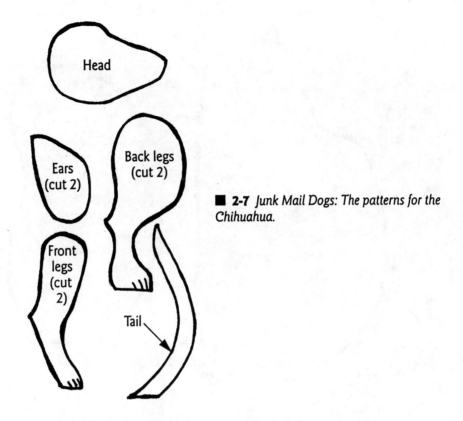

■ **2-7** *Junk Mail Dogs: The patterns for the Chihuahua.*

- The dachshund (Figs. 2-8 and 2-9) is made from a long business envelope 4 × 9½ inches.
- The poodle (Figs. 2-10 and 2-11) is made from a greeting card envelope 4½ × 5¾ inches. Glue cotton onto each pouf indicated on the patterns.

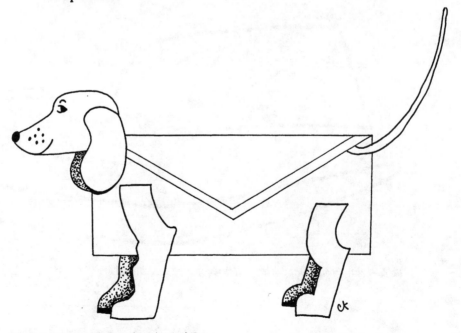

■ **2-8** *The Dachshund Junk Mail Dog.*

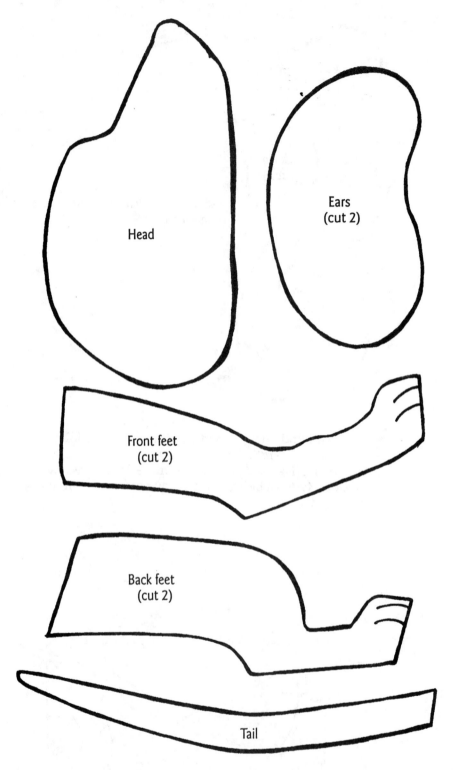

Head

Ears
(cut 2)

Front feet
(cut 2)

Back feet
(cut 2)

Tail

■ **2-9** *Junk Mail Dogs: The patterns for the Dachshund.*

■ **2-10** *The Poodle Junk Mail Dog.*

- The dalmatian (Figs. 2-12 and 2-13) is made from a greeting card envelope 5 × 7 inches.
- The Saint Bernard (Figs. 2-14, 2-15, and 2-16) is made from a large manila envelope 9 × 12 inches.

3. Color the envelopes with crayons. Stuff them lightly with tissue paper or crumpled newspaper. Tape them closed.

4. Cut out the heads, ears, tails, and legs. Color them. Glue them onto the envelope bodies. Stand the dogs up after the glue has dried.

☞ *Making a book about dogs*

🔎 *Categorizing; recording information*
Start a book of photographs, magazine pictures, or pictures of dogs that the children draw. You can categorize the dogs according to the type, color, size, name, and so on.

Pet pause *What is a "litter"? A litter is a group of puppies born at one time from the same mother.*

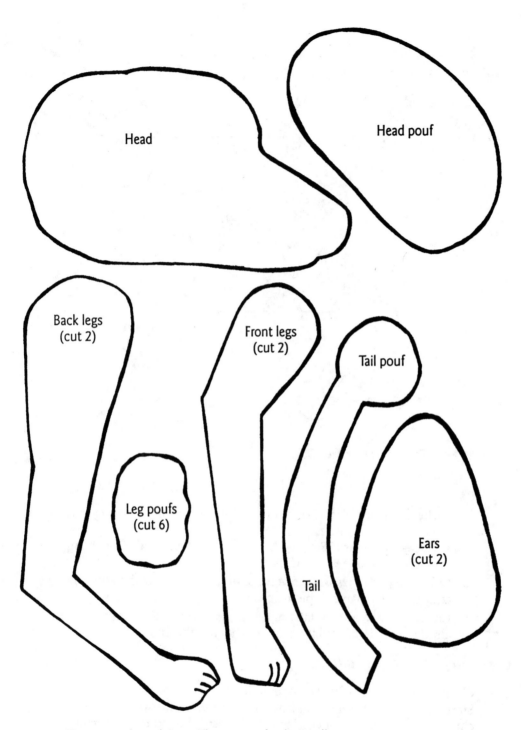

■ **2-11** *Junk Mail Dogs: The patterns for the Poodle.*

■ **2-12** *The Dalmation Junk Mail Dog.*

 Making a graph

Recording information; using numbers
Make different types of graphs using information about the children's dogs.

1. Yes/No Graph
   "Do you have a dog for a pet?" Write *Yes* on one sheet of paper and *No* on another sheet. Let the children write their names under the correct word for them. Count the number of names.

2. Bar Graphs
   Create bar graphs by using the colors of their dogs, sizes, ages, and so forth.

Rap
"The Junk Mail Dog"
Dogs come in different shapes and sizes.
Junk mail dog, junk mail dog.
Full of fun and full of surprises.
Junk mail dog, junk mail dog.
Friendly pal, loyal friend.
Junk mail dog, junk mail dog.
From the beginning to the end.
Junk mail dog, junk mail dog.
Yeah!

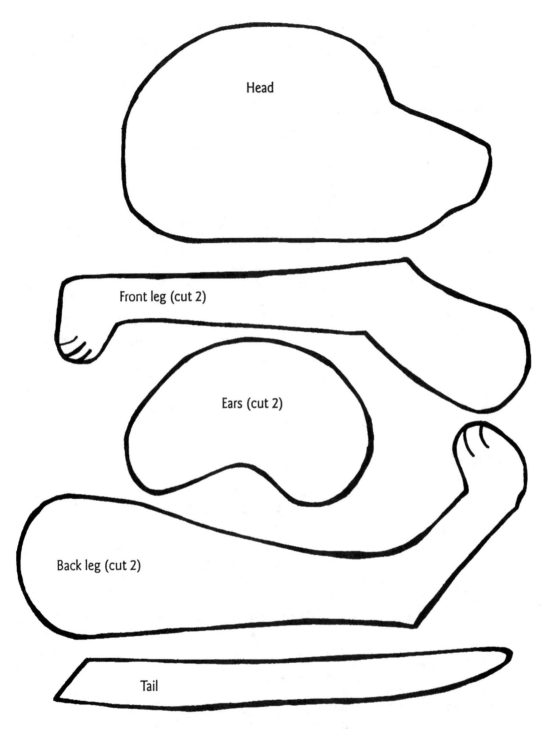

Head

Front leg (cut 2)

Ears (cut 2)

Back leg (cut 2)

Tail

■ **2-13** *Junk Mail Dogs: The patterns for the Dalmation.*

■ **2-14** *The Saint Bernard Junk Mail Dog.*

Dogs have two ears, two eyes, and a nose, but all of these are various shapes and sizes depending on the kind of dog. Some dogs have ears that are pointed and stand up; other dogs have ears that are long and hang down. Dogs have whiskers.

☞ *Looking at a dog*

🔍 *Observing; manipulating materials; asking questions; finding information; recording information*
Try to arrange for another dog to visit the children. Encourage the children to be gentle and quiet as they observe the dog. Let children pet the dog if it seems safe to do so. Talk about the ears, eyes, and nose. Talk about the color of the dog and the length of its hair. Encourage the children to ask questions.

Let children look through books about dogs and the section of the *D* encyclopedia on dogs. Talk about the different kinds of ears, eyes, and noses.

At the easel in the art center, let children paint dog faces. The children might enjoy drawing and coloring pictures of dogs, also.

☞ *Word picture*

🔍 *Classifying; recording information*
The teacher can draw an outline of a dog on a large sheet of bulletin board paper. The children can then write the name of the dog's body part along the outline. They should write the word repeatedly until they come to the next body part. Each body part can be written in a different color. Let the children decide the words that should be used. Younger children might say head, body, tail, feet. older children might include more specific names such as nose, toes, and whiskers.

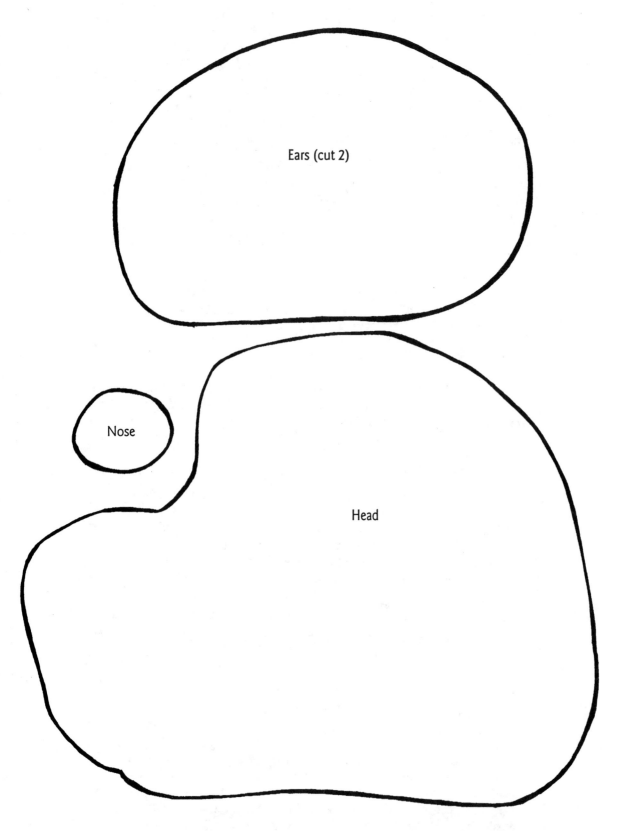

Ears (cut 2)

Nose

Head

■ 2-15 *Junk Mail Dogs: The patterns for the Saint Bernard head, ears, and nose.*

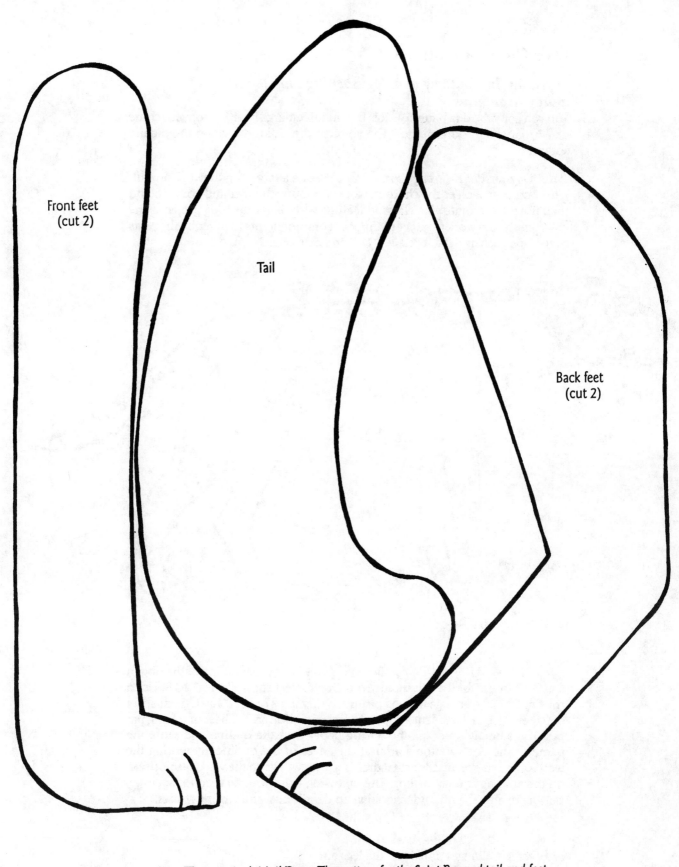

Front feet
(cut 2)

Tail

Back feet
(cut 2)

■ **2-16** *Junk Mail Dogs: The pattern for the Saint Bernard tail and feet.*

Let's Create a Word Dog

🔍 *Learning the anatomy of a dog; spelling and definition of anatomical terms*

You can copy the dog pattern as it is or you can enlarge it with a copy machine or with an overhead projector. The younger the child, the larger the picture should be.

Word Dog for Pre-K through First Grade Create a large dog drawing on bulletin board paper. Let the children work in groups to label and color it, and then use it to decorate your classroom along with their other dog projects. The children should work together to think of common terms to describe the parts of the dog such as head, back, leg, tail, and ears (Fig. 2-17).

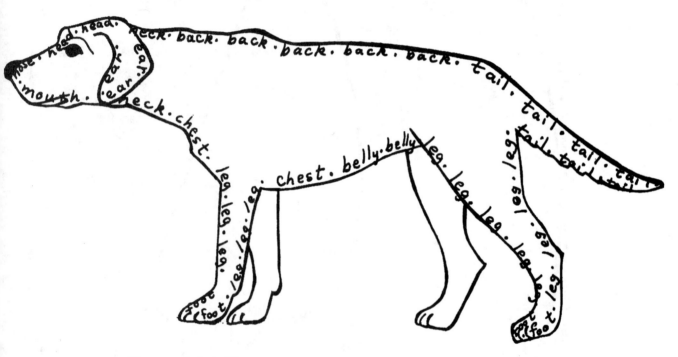

■ **2-17** *The Word Dog.*

Advanced Word Dog for Grades Two and Three Trace the outline of the dog in Fig. 2-17 to use for the Advanced Word Dog project shown in Fig. 2-18. Use a copy machine to enlarge the dog picture so that it fits on an 8½-×-11-inch sheet of paper. Give each student a copy of the dog outline and a sheet of tracing paper. The students can tape the tracing paper over the outline and write the name of the dog's anatomy around the edges of the outline. By writing the word over and over on the actual drawing, they will learn the word, its position on the animal, and its spelling. The following words can be used for spelling, putting in alphabetical order, looking up definitions, and writing stories.

1. *Brisket* The lower chest of an animal
2. *Crest* The top of the head
3. *Feathers* Fringes of hair on the legs and tail

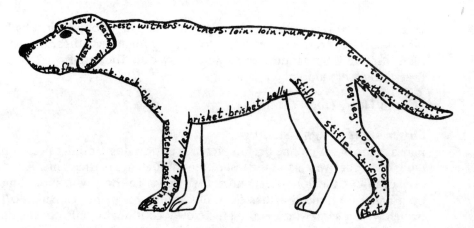

■ **2-18** *An example of the Advanced Word Dog.*

4. *Flews*   A dog's upper lip
5. *Hock*   The ankle of an animal
6. *Leather*   A dog's ear that hangs down
7. *Loin*   The lower back of an animal
8. *Muzzle*   The long jaws and nose of an animal (snout)
9. *Pastern*   The leg of an animal
10. *Withers*   The shoulders of an animal

Word Dog
When you write the parts of a dog around the edges of a drawing, you can create a dog made only of words.

What you need
☐ Picture of the word dog
☐ Pencil
☐ Crayons to color the word dog

Directions
1. Use a pencil to write the names of the dog's body parts around the edges of the word dog.
2. Color the word dog lightly with crayons so the words show through the coloring.

☞ **Further study**

🔍 *Designing investigations*
Dogs are part of the same family that includes wolves, coyotes, and foxes. Help children brainstorm ways to find out more about these animals. After the children have found out some information, use a Venn diagram to discuss the similarities and differences.

Dogs have four legs. Dogs have four toes on each foot. Each toe has a blunt claw. Each paw has a cushioned pad covered with skin that is tough.

Dogs can smell very well. They can recognize people or objects just by how they smell. Dogs can hear very well, too. A dog might even hear its owner's car in traffic. Dogs cannot see as well as we can. They cannot see colors. Everything looks kind of grayish to them.

☞ *"Come Here, Dog" Game*

🔍 *Observing through listening*

Play a game in which one person pretends to be a dog, another person pretends to be the owner, and the rest of the children are participants. The children can sit on the floor or remain at their desks. The dog, who should make up a name for himself or herself, walks among his or her classmates. The owner, who is somewhere among the crowd, continually calls out the dog's name softly while the other children softly say "come here, dog." The dog wanders through the crowd and tries to find his or her owner by listening for his or her name. When the dog finds the owner, the teacher picks a new dog and owner. If the game needs to proceed more quickly, start with two or more dogs, all with different names and different owners.

Dogs "talk" to us and each other by making different kinds of sounds. Dogs bark, growl, howl, yelp, and whine. Dogs communicate by wagging their tails, by looking at you in certain ways, or by doing certain things with their bodies, like lying down if you speak loudly to them or running to meet you when they see you.

💡 *Sharing dog experiences*

🔍 *Communicating information*

"Tell us about sounds your dog makes. What do these sounds mean? Do you talk to your dog? Do you think he understands what you are saying? How can you tell? What are some things your dog does to communicate with you?"

☞ *Dramatic play*

🔍 *Communicating information*

Allow children to pretend to be dogs and act out how dogs bark, growl, howl, yelp, and whine.

☞ *Words and sounds*

Onomatopoeia is a poetic device in which words sound like their meanings. *Crash* and *boom* are examples. *Growl* and *bark* are words that sound like their meanings, too.

Let children write a poem using these words and any other words that sound like their meaning.

Dogs need a balanced diet so that they grow and develop in a healthy way. Dog food is sold in bags and cans in grocery stores and pet stores. Dogs might enjoy foods that you eat, like hamburger meat or cheese or eggs, but the best food for them is their own dog food. Puppies should be fed small amounts of food three or four times a day. A grown dog should eat once or twice a day. Dogs always need fresh water in their bowl.

Dogs like special treats like dog biscuits. You can give them a dog biscuit for a snack or as a reward for doing something good.

☞ *The value of cooking with children*

🔍 *Working with fractions; measuring; observing chemical reactions*
When we cook with children, we introduce them to the wonderful experience of hands-on chemistry and math. As children cook the following dog and people foods, they gain first-hand knowledge of fractions, the importance of accurate measuring, and the meaning of dry versus liquid measure. They create mixtures and encounter chemical reactions as the individual ingredients change into a totally new substance.

In addition, the students have an opportunity to classify ingredients as solids or liquids (An egg can be both, depending on whether it is cooked or raw). Older students should list ingredients according to the amount of each in the recipe. This method necessitates measuring and perhaps weighing each one to discover "which is more."

When cooking with children, always consider their safety first. An adult must supervise all activities, making certain that the children are not harmed by hot stoves or sharp utensils.

Let's Create Baked Dog Biscuits

🔍 *Learning about dry measure and liquid measure; using whole numbers and fractions; learning to follow directions*
These dog biscuits taste like rye crackers and are so good that you might want to try a few yourself (Fig. 2-19)! Squirrels, cockatiels, and hamsters like them, too.

■ **2-19** *Baked Dog Biscuits.*

What you need

- ☐ ¼ cup warm water
- ☐ One package dry yeast
- ☐ 3 cups canned chicken broth, undiluted
- ☐ 4 teaspoons salt
- ☐ ¼ cup molasses
- ☐ 1½ cups rye flour
- ☐ 2 cups oatmeal
- ☐ 1 cup cornmeal
- ☐ 4 cups flour
- ☐ One egg (for glazing)
- ☐ Large bowl
- ☐ Wooden spoon
- ☐ Breadboard
- ☐ Rolling pin
- ☐ Cookie cutter
- ☐ Greased baking sheets

Directions

1. Assemble all the ingredients. Divide them into two groups. Group number one should be solids. Group number two should be liquids. Make a list of the ingredients that are solids and the ingredients that are liquids. Older students can list the ingredients in order according to amount, from most to least. You can use these lists when you create a box for the dog biscuits. Now you are ready to cook.
2. Pour the warm water into the bowl. Add the dry yeast and stir.
3. Add the chicken broth, salt, molasses, rye flour, oatmeal, cornmeal, and flour. Mix it until a dough forms.
4. Roll out the dough ½-inch thick on the breadboard. Cut it into shapes with a cookie cutter.
5. Put the dog biscuits close together on the greased baking sheet.
6. To make the glaze, break an egg into a jar. Add 1 tablespoon water. Put a lid on the jar and shake it like crazy. Brush the egg glaze on each biscuit.
7. Bake at 325°F for 30 minutes until light brown.

Yield: 76 2-inch dog biscuits

Let's Create a Box for the Dog Biscuits

Record data; classify solids and liquids; list ingredients according to amount; use descriptive terms

Decorate an empty cereal or cracker box to hold the baked dog biscuits.

What you need

- ☐ Empty cereal box or cracker box
- ☐ Construction paper to cover the box
- ☐ Scissors

☐ White glue
☐ Markers

Directions

1. Cover the box with construction paper. Design an attractive new cover for your dog biscuits. Include the following information:
   - Picture of a dog
   - The name of the dog biscuits
   - Description of the dog biscuits that will make people want to buy them for their dog.
2. On the box, list the ingredients in two rows as either solids or liquids. Older students can list the ingredients in order according to amount from most to least. You might need to measure and perhaps weigh each ingredient to discover which is present in the greater quantity.
3. Store the biscuits in the box.

A note to the adult There are no right or wrong answers as to which ingredient is present in the greater quantity. The purpose of this activity is for the students to gain insight into weighing and measuring. The students should reach a consensus on the order in which the ingredients should be listed.

 A visit from a veterinarian

 Asking questions

Ask a veterinarian to come for a visit. Encourage the children to ask questions like: "Do a dog's teeth need to be brushed?" The teacher should let children formulate some possible questions prior to the visit. The veterinarian might want to talk to the children about spaying and neutering.

To stay healthy, a dog needs regular visits to the veterinarian. The veterinarian will talk to you about taking care of your dog and will give it medicines to keep it from getting certain diseases. He or she can also tell you how to care for your dog's teeth. You should never use regular "people" toothpaste on your dog's teeth because fluoride is not good for them. Dogs have their own brands of toothpaste, which are available at your veterinarian's office.

Brushing a dog's hair helps keep it neat and clean. If a dog has short hair, it might only need brushing once a week, but a dog with long hair might need brushing once each day. Sometimes a dog needs a bath. Dogs can be bathed with warm water and special soap for dogs. *Grooming* is a word that means brushing and cleaning.

 Setting up a dog clinic

 Classifying; manipulating materials; measuring; using numbers; communicating and recording information; applying knowledge

Let children set up a "dog clinic" in the dramatic play area. Children can bring toy dogs from home to be the patients. Provide a telephone, appointment book, files, bandages, empty containers for pretend medicine, and any other materials for pretend play.

Most dogs respond to their names and come running when you call them. Dogs can be trained to follow your commands, like to sit or shake hands.

Dogs respond to many words you say. Dogs seem to understand many words and sentences and also understand your tone of voice (if you sound happy or unhappy). Some dogs are trained to be in movies and on television.

Dogs are smart

Communicating information
"What are some things your dogs can do? How do you talk to your dog? What are some things your dog can understand?"

Dogs in movies

Communicating information
Bring movies to class in which dogs play an important role. Watch the movies and talk about the actions the dogs perform.

A dog that lives indoors might like to sleep in a special bed made for dogs or might choose to sleep on the floor. Some dogs are allowed to sleep on the furniture or even in a regular bed. Dogs who live outdoors need a safe, warm shelter to protect them from the weather. A doghouse is one type of shelter. You can put blankets in the doghouse so that your dog has a soft, warm place to sleep.

Let's Create a Game for *Harry the Dirty Dog*

Developing observational skills and directional vocabulary by following a map; communicating information by mapping; creating a model of **Harry the Dirty Dog**

Harry starts his day as a white dog with black spots. Create your own dog by using a large dried lima bean and a black marker. Then use the map to take him on Harry's adventures.

What you need
☐ The children's book, *Harry the Dirty Dog* by Gene Zion
☐ Crayons or colored pencils
☐ Large dry lima bean
☐ Black permanent marker
☐ Street map (Ask a realtor to donate maps.)
☐ Paper for drawing more maps

Directions
1. Read the story, *Harry the Dirty Dog* by Gene Zion.
2. The map in Fig. 2-20 can be copied and enlarged on a copy machine. Color the map lightly with crayons or pencils.
3. To create Harry, use the black permanent marker to draw ears, paws, eyes, nose, and spots on the lima bean (Fig. 2-21).
4. Using directional words, walk Harry around the neighborhood to the different sites mentioned in the story. Some words to use might be *left*, *right*, *north*, *south*, *up*, and *down*.
5. Locate streets on a real map. What are their names and where do they go?

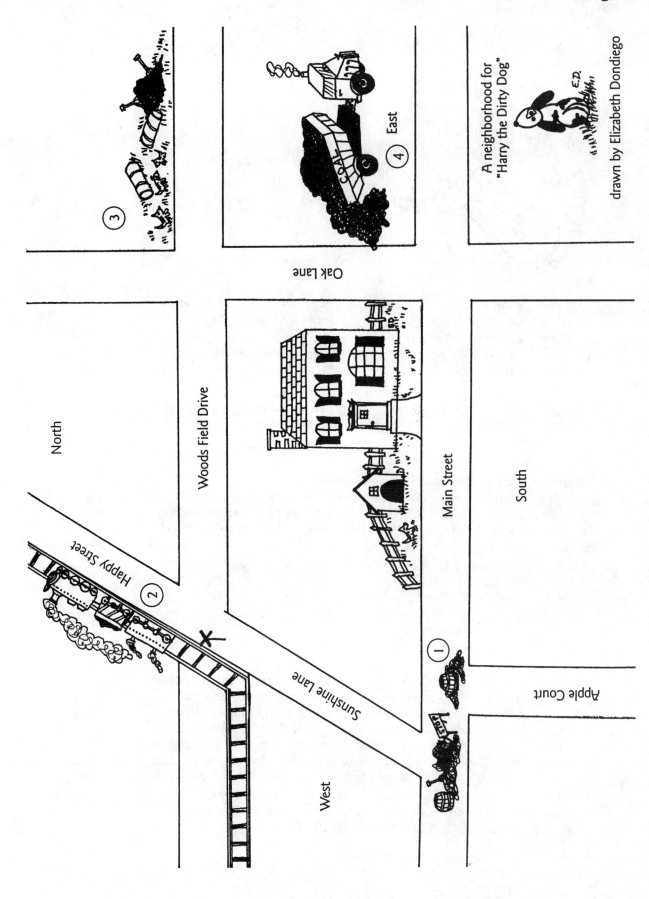

A neighborhood for
"Harry the Dirty Dog"

E.D.

drawn by Elizabeth Dondiego

North

West

East

South

Woods Field Drive

Happy Street

Sunshine Lane

Main Street

Oak Lane

Apple Court

COAL

① ② ③ ④

STOP

■ **2-20** *A map for Harry the Dirty Dog. Use with a lima bean dog.*

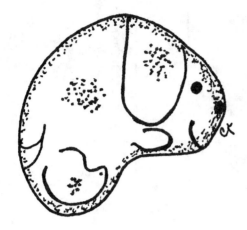

■ **2-21** *A lima bean made into Harry the Dirty Dog.*

6. Walk around inside your school. Draw a map that shows how to get to places such as the main office, the lunch room, and the media center. Take Harry on a trip using your school map.

7. Draw a map of your own neighborhood or street. Show how to get from one place to another. Trade maps with a friend. Can other people follow your map?

Take good care of your dog and give it plenty of love and attention. Walk with it, play with it, and enjoy your special friend. Dogs live about 12 to 16 years.

☞ *Closure*

 Applying knowledge; drawing conclusions

Bringing closure to your study is important. Review your initial goals and give children opportunities to talk about what they have learned and how they are using what they have learned. Here are some ideas to help bring closure to your study:

1. Let children write a cinquain about dogs or a certain type of dog. A *cinquain* is composed of five lines:
   • One word for the title
   • Two words to describe the title
   • Three words to express action
   • Four words to express feeling
   • The title again

2. Plan a dog show using the dogs you have created throughout this study. This activity can be like a puppet show. Turn a large table on its side so that children can get behind it and hold their dogs up so the audience can see. Each child can show his or her dog, tell about it, let it do tricks, or whatever you decide. Let the children create awards or ribbons to give to the dogs (friendliest dog, cutest dog, most creative dog, smartest dog, best behaved dog, etc.). Make sure that each dog gets a ribbon or award.

3. Children can conduct interviews (telephone or in person) with veterinarians, groomers, dog trainers, or pet store owners. They can collect this information to present to the class.

4. Children can bring in videotapes of their dogs. Have a special video day and eat no-bake "people" cookies while you watch the videos. Children could write stories to go with their videos.

5. Children could create a video at home entitled *A Dog's View of the World*. To make this video, they would need to take the camera down to the dog's eye level, crawl around, and pretend the camera is a dog.

6. You can read some fiction storybooks to the children. Look for more stories about dogs like *Harry the Dirty Dog* and share them.

Let's Create No-Bake "People" Cookies

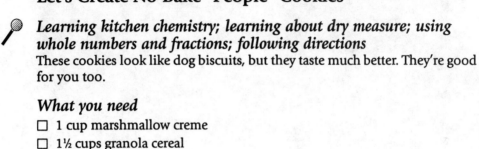

Learning kitchen chemistry; learning about dry measure; using whole numbers and fractions; following directions
These cookies look like dog biscuits, but they taste much better. They're good for you too.

What you need
- ☐ 1 cup marshmallow creme
- ☐ 1½ cups granola cereal
- ☐ ¼ cup raisins
- ☐ 1 cup graham cracker crumbs
- ☐ Large bowl
- ☐ Wooden spoon
- ☐ Breadboard
- ☐ Rolling pin
- ☐ Cookie cutter

Directions
1. Measure the marshmallow creme, granola cereal, and raisins into the bowl. Mix them together to make a dough.
2. Pour the graham cracker crumbs and the dough onto the breadboard.
3. Roll the dough out ½-inch thick. Cut it into shapes with a cookie cutter. Put the no-bake "people" cookies on a plate.

Yield: 18 2-inch "people" cookies

MICE,
HAMSTERS,
& GERBILS

Science goals

To help children become aware of what these animals are like, how they behave as pets, and how we can take care of them

Teacher/Parent planning

Think about how you can get one or more of these animals to the class for a visit. Send a letter home asking for parents to send pictures of or bring these animals if they have one of them for a pet. Perhaps a local pet store might be willing to bring them for a visit. Borrow informational books from the library. Prepare to write words about the animals you are studying on a large sheet of chart paper.

Materials needed for discussion and activities

☐ Live animals for observation
☐ Informational books from the library

Related words

rodent A group of mammals having sharp front teeth that keep growing and must be worn away by gnawing

gnaw To bite or chew away little by little

pellet A small, hard ball (or other shape) made of dry food

instinct Something an animal does naturally. The animal does not have to be taught how to do it.

Scientists organize all living things into groups. Mice, hamsters, and gerbils belong to a group called mammals. Mammals have hair or fur, a backbone, are warm-blooded, feed milk to their babies, and breathe with lungs. They can also be rodents, which means that they have special front teeth adapted for gnawing and nibbling. These teeth are called incisors. Rodents have two top and two bottom incisors, but they also have back teeth for chewing. The incisors allow rodents to gnaw wood or break the shells of nuts. These teeth grow throughout the animal's life.

Other than mice, hamsters, and gerbils, some rodents that you might have heard of are beavers, chipmunks, squirrels, gophers, guinea pigs, porcupines, woodchucks, and rabbits.

Mice are the smallest rodents. Hamsters and gerbils are also small. In the wild, foxes and owls often try to catch rodents that are too small to fight back. These rodents try to hide from larger animals. Sometimes they run under rocks or dig tunnels under the ground. They build nests to live in safely. Hiding, digging, and building are instincts. Rodents also have an instinct to explore, which helps them find food. They explore new places and things by sniffing, by nibbling, or by running through or around objects.

A 10-gallon aquarium makes a good home for a mouse, hamster, or gerbil. You need a wire-mesh cover for the top. Bedding needs to be placed on the bottom of the cage. Types of bedding include wood chips or shavings, hay, or shredded paper without any print on it. These pets often help make their bedding by shredding up soft, clean fabric, tissue, bathroom tissue rolls, or packaged nesting material. Their cage needs to be cleaned about twice a week. Do not put the cage near a window or where cold air can blow on the animal. These pets are nocturnal, which means they are more active at night and sleep a lot during the day.

These animals can be held and petted. These animals have four legs and hold their food in their front paws when they eat. They wash their faces, whiskers, and paws after they eat.

 ### Visiting with a mouse, hamster, or gerbil

 ### Observing

If a parent has brought the mouse, hamster, or gerbil let the parent tell about it as the children observe it in its cage or as the parent holds it. Ask the parent to talk about how they got the pet, where it stays, what it eats, and how it acts. Discuss the cage, the bedding, the care of the animal.

Encourage the children to look at the ears, eyes, nose, and tail. Write some descriptive words on the chart paper.

 ### Sharing

 ### Communicating information

"If you have a mouse, hamster, or gerbil for a pet, where did you get it? Tell us what your mouse, hamster, or gerbil looks like." If the children have brought pictures of their pets, let them show the pictures now.

Mice

A mouse is a small animal with a pointed face, round black or red eyes, rounded ears that stand up, and a thin tail. There are hundreds of kinds of mice. Scientists use some kinds of mice to help us learn about diseases and the effects of drugs, and to conduct experiments about behavior.

A house mouse is a kind of mouse that can be a good pet. You can get a mouse from a pet store. You can choose from many different colors like white, brown, black, gray, red, pink, cream, or mixtures of these colors.

A mouse is always busy. It stands up to sniff the air. It runs, jumps, and climbs. Usually, the only time a mouse stops moving is when it curls up into a ball to sleep.

A grown mouse is about 3 to 4 inches long. A baby mouse can fit in a teaspoon and weighs less than a penny. A baby mouse is called a pup, and the pups are called a litter, just as with dogs. The mother is called a doe, and the father is called a buck.

A mouse has poor eyesight, but it has a good sense of smell and keen hearing. A mouse has whiskers, which, from tip to tip, are about as long as its body. With its whiskers, a mouse can feel objects and find its way through narrow places.

A mouse has five toes on its back feet and four toes on its front feet. The fifth toe works something like a person's thumb. A mouse has 16 teeth, 4 incisors, and 12 molars. Having hard things to chew on is important for a mouse because its incisors keep growing throughout its life.

Mice need plenty of water. You can use a water dish, or you can get a special water bottle from the pet store. Mice should be fed different kinds of seeds. Seed mixes can be purchased at a pet store. Mice like fruits and vegetables, such as lettuce, carrots, and apples. Feed them very small pieces and remove whatever is not eaten within 15 minutes. Moldy foods can make your mouse sick. Mice really do like cheese, but they should only have a little bit once in a while because cheese has a lot of fat in it. Did you know that mice like dog biscuits? Chewing on the biscuits is good for their teeth.

Mice need exercise. They play with toys to work out. An exercise wheel is good for them. Tubes from bathroom tissue are fun for them to run through and sleep in. Mice like to climb in and out of small boxes.

Mice are easily frightened, so they must be handled gently. One way to pick up a mouse is to hold its tail near the base and quickly lift it. Never grab the tip of the tail because the skin might come off. If a mouse will come onto your hand, cover it with your other hand.

Mice can be trained. Young mice are easier to train than older mice, and females are easier to train than males. To work with a mouse, put it on top of the wire-mesh cage or a table. Mice are afraid of heights and will probably not jump off. A mouse can learn such tricks as sitting up for food, climbing a ladder, jumping through a hoop, or running through a maze. You can train it by using foods like sunflower seeds as a reward and coaxing it where you want it to go.

A mouse keeps its body clean by licking itself all over. It wets its paws and washes its whiskers. It washes behind its ears. It uses its nails to comb its fur.

Mice can be wonderful pets. They live about two years.

Pet pause *Mice originally came from Asia. Mice followed people because they could find food more easily by living near people. Mice probably came to the United States aboard ships in the 1500s. Mice have spread all over the world because of their skill in climbing aboard ships that are roped to harbor docks.*

Let's Create Teardrop Mouse and Little Books

Becoming familiar with the anatomy of a mouse by creating a model; manipulating materials; using reference material; recording data

Turn a teardrop shape and a paper plate into a flat mouse (Fig. 3-1). Put a rubber band around its middle to fatten it up.

What you need to make the Teardrop Mouse

☐ 9-inch white paper plate
☐ Construction paper
☐ Scissors
☐ White glue
☐ Paper punch
☐ Crayons
☐ Markers
☐ Tape
☐ Rubber band (optional)

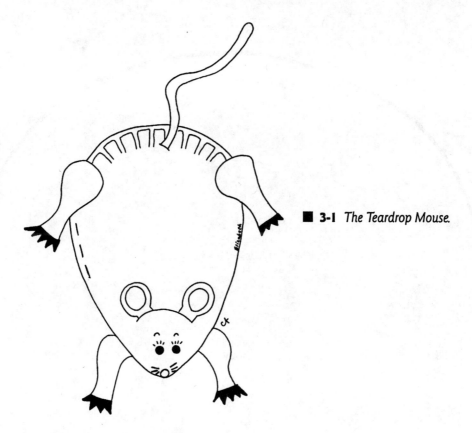

■ **3-1** *The Teardrop Mouse.*

Directions

1. Trace and cut out the teardrop mouse body pattern in Fig. 3-2. Lay the pattern on the paper plate so that the large end of the teardrop is even with the edge of the plate. Draw around the pattern and cut out the mouse body. Have an adult help you cut the slit shown on the pattern.

2. Use the patterns in Fig. 3-3 to trace and cut out the mouse ears, legs, and tail from construction paper.

3. Use crayons to color the mouse. Glue paper-punch eyes and nose on it. Use a marker to draw on whiskers.

4. Insert the ears in the slit. Tape them in place under the body. Glue the front legs, back legs, and tail on the body.

5. After the glue dries, put a rubber band around the mouse's middle overnight to make him more round.

6. In the media center or library, find some books about real mice and about imaginary mice. Write or dictate a story about your mouse. Make a mouse Little Book.

What you need to make Little Books

☐ Typing paper or notebook paper
☐ Stapler
☐ Colored pencils for grades two and three

Directions

Use the teardrop pattern in Fig. 3-2 to cut out pages for a little book. Make as many pages as you need for your book. Staple them together, using your teardrop mouse as the book cover.

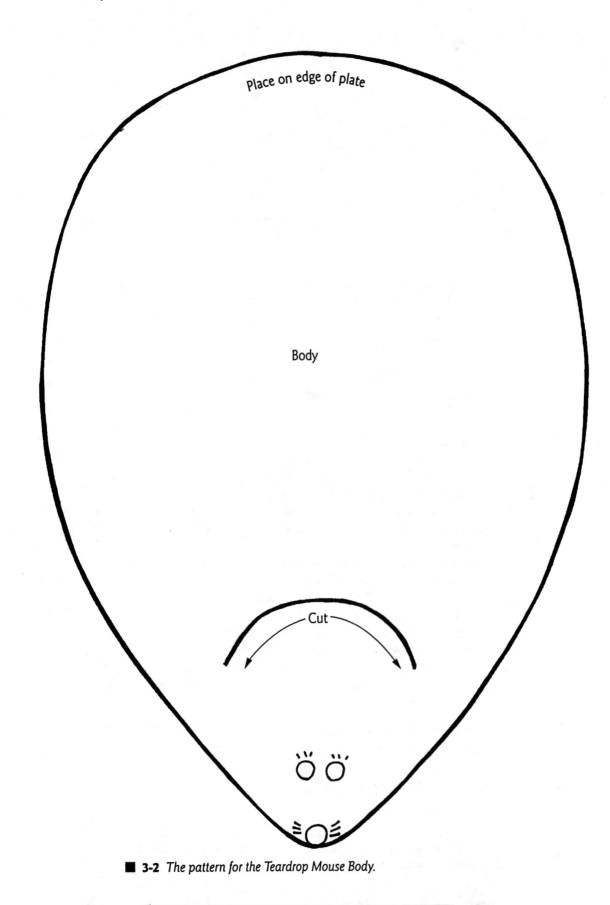

Place on edge of plate

Body

Cut

■ **3-2** *The pattern for the Teardrop Mouse Body.*

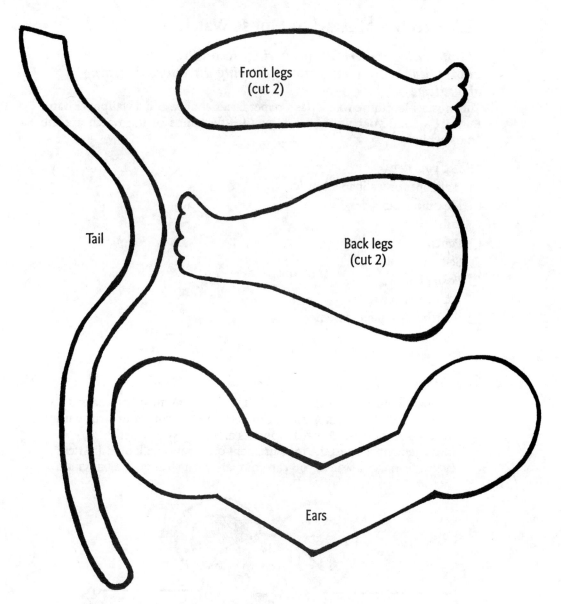

Front legs
(cut 2)

Tail

Back legs
(cut 2)

Ears

■ **3-3** *The patterns for the Teardrop Mouse legs, tail, and ears.*

For Pre-K through First Grade Make the pages out of typing paper. Draw pictures and write as many words as you can to tell your mouse story.

For Grades Two and Three Make the pages out of lined paper. Write a story about your mouse on the pages. Use colored pencils to illustrate your story by drawing large, lightly colored pictures on top of the words.

For Older Students Use reference material to write a report on mice. Find out where mice live. What do they eat? Do they have enemies? Who are their enemies? If you had a pet mouse, how would you take care of him? Write your report about mice on an index card. Glue the card to the underside of your teardrop mouse to create a mouse report.

Let's Create a Mustachio Mouse Watch

Manipulating materials; measuring; recording numerical information with a bar graph; following directions; learning about time

The mustachio mouse watch has a paper fastener nose and a wallpaper band that fits around your wrist. The big and little hands of the watch are the "mustachio."

What you need
- ☐ Wallpaper or wallpaper border
- ☐ Measuring tape
- ☐ Ruler
- ☐ Pencil
- ☐ Scissors
- ☐ Poster board
- ☐ Paper punch
- ☐ ½-inch metal paper fastener
- ☐ Markers
- ☐ Crayons

Directions
1. To make a mustachio mouse watch (Fig. 3-4), you must first make a wristband that fits you. A friend can help you measure your wrist with the measuring tape. How many inches around is your wrist measurement? Record the measurement on a class chalk board. After everyone makes a watch, you can compare wrist sizes with a bar graph.

■ **3-4** *The Mustachio Mouse Watch.*

2. Add 1½ inches to your wrist size. Use the wristband pattern in Fig. 3-5, a pencil, and a ruler to draw the wristband on wallpaper. (The length you make the wristband pattern will depend on the size of your wrist.) Cut the wristband out. Cut a ½-inch slit in side A as the pattern shows.

3. Use the patterns in Fig. 3-5 to draw the watch and the big and little hands onto poster board. Cut them out. Use a paper punch to make a hole in each one.

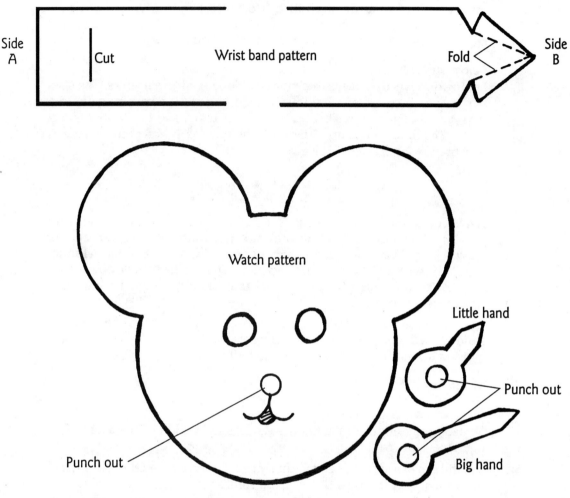

■ 3-5 *The patterns for the Mustachio Mouse Watch.*

4. Use markers to write numbers on your watch, to color the big and little hands, and to draw the mouse eyes and mouth. Color the rest of the watch and the band with crayons.

5. To assemble the watch, insert the paper fastener through the little hand, the big hand, the mouse nose, and then through a little hole punched in the wrist band. Open the paper fastener under the band.

6. Put the watch on your wrist. Have a friend help you fold the edges of side B down so it will fit through the slit in side A. Open the edges of side B to hold the band in place.

Make a horizontal bar graph
Students can measure and cut out a paper rectangle that is 2 inches wide and long enough to fit around their wrists. How long is each rectangle? Help them record this number on their paper strip.

Make a chart of poster board entitled "How Large Are Our Wrists?" Write the children's names on the left side of the chart. Each child can glue his or her rectangle beside his or her name, creating a horizontal bar graph.

Learning to tell time

During the class day, certain activities are done at different times. The class schedule with corresponding times should be posted where everyone can read it easily. For example, recess might be at 10:00, and lunch might be at 12:15. The children can practice setting the time of day on their watches as they prepare for different activities.

Hamsters

Hamsters are small, furry rodents. Their bodies are plump and round. They come in different colors such as brown, beige, white, black, and shades of red. Their fur is very soft. Pet hamsters are about 4 to 7 inches long. Pet stores usually have several types of hamsters. One type is called a teddy bear hamster. An Angora hamster is another type that has very long fur. Some other types are golden hamsters and Siberian hamsters.

Hamsters have bright black eyes and long whiskers. They have pointed noses and rounded ears. They have very short tails, which are about ½ inch long. A hamster has short legs, so it waddles when it walks.

 Waddling

Drawing conclusions

"What other kinds of animals have short legs and waddle? Does a duck waddle? Does a penguin?"

Conduct an experiment. Let one child at a time walk across the room standing up straight. Time this. Then let each child squat down and waddle across the room. Time this. Talk about the difference between the two times. Give the children the opportunity to explain their conclusions on why the times are different.

Hamsters can squeeze through very small places. They often hide. Hamsters cannot climb as well as mice. They do not see well in the daytime, so you have to be very careful when handling them. They can fall from your hand or fall off a table.

A hamster has a pouch in each of its cheeks. A hamster picks up food with its paws, then stuffs the food inside these pouches. A hamster's instinct is to hide some of its food. It might also leave the food in the pouches to eat later. Wild hamsters hide food because they are saving it for winter. They want to be sure to have enough food during cold weather. Hamsters eat seeds, food pellets that you can buy from a pet store, and fresh foods such as lettuce and apples. Fresh foods rot quickly so you have to find a hamster's hiding place to remove any uneaten fresh foods. Hamsters need water in their cages. You can use a little water dish or buy a special bottle from the pet store.

It is best to pick up a hamster from behind. Don't try to pick it up while it is eating or building a nest. It might bite you.

Let's Create a Paper Bag Hamster Puppet

Observing and recreating an animal; manipulating materials, following directions

The paper bag hamster has big teeth and a short, stubby tail (Fig. 3-6). With your help, it can do a lot of things that a real hamster can't do, such as sing, dance, and talk!

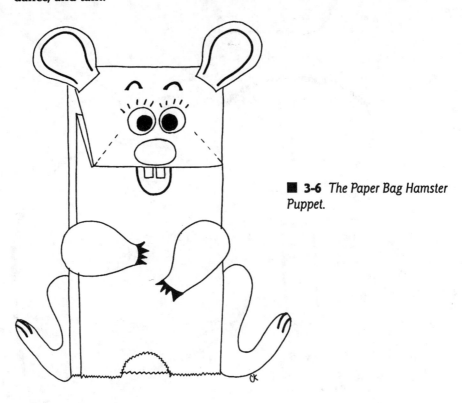

■ **3-6** *The Paper Bag Hamster Puppet.*

What you need

☐ Brown, yellow, and pink construction paper
☐ White poster paper
☐ Scissors
☐ White glue
☐ Brown paper lunch bag
☐ Markers
☐ Crayons

Directions

1. Use the patterns in Fig. 3-7 to trace the following pieces onto the construction paper: a pink nose, two yellow eyes, two brown ears, two brown front legs, and two brown back legs.

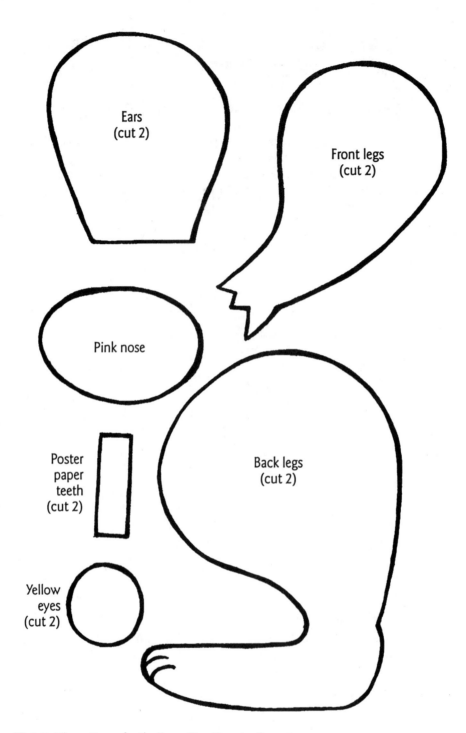

■ 3-7 *The patterns for the Paper Bag Hamster Puppet.*

 2. Cut two front teeth from white poster paper.

3. Glue the two front legs on the front of the paper bag. (The side with the flap is the front of the bag.) Glue the two back legs on the back of the bag so they can be seen from the front. Use a marker or crayons to draw paws.

4. Glue the two ears on the top of the flap. Glue the two eyes in the middle of the flap. Use crayons or markers to add eyeballs and eyelashes.

5. Glue the pink nose at the edge of the flap, below the eyes. Glue the two teeth under the flap so they can be seen beneath the nose.

6. Use a marker to draw a mouth under the teeth. Draw a short, stubby tail on the back of the puppet.

7. To play with your puppet after the glue dries, insert your hand in the bag and bend your fingers so they fit into the flap. Move your fingers up and down to make your puppet's mouth open and close.

Hamsters need exercise. A safe way to let a hamster run is on an exercise wheel inside the cage or attached to the cage. Hamsters enjoy sleeping in small boxes or little houses, which can be purchased at the pet store. They like to feel cozy, safe, and warm.

A hamster can be a wonderful pet and friend. Hamsters live about three or four years.

Gerbils

Gerbils make good pets. They are known for being gentle and easy to care for. Most gerbils are a brownish color, but you can get black, white, golden, and even lilac gerbils. An adult gerbil is about 4 inches long. They have long, furry tails. In fact, a gerbil's tail is about as long as its body. Their fur is kind of oily, so they do not feel as fluffy as hamsters.

A gerbil has four legs. The back legs are longer and stronger than the front ones. A gerbil uses its back legs to make leaps and bounds, much like a kangaroo. It walks on all four legs, but it often stands up on its back legs and uses its tail for balance. It often stands up just to look around.

Gerbils are quiet, but sometimes they give soft squeaks. They are active during the day and night, but they are especially active at night.

Gerbils are desert animals. They came originally from Mongolia, a desert area between northern China and Siberia. They do not need a lot of water, but you need to give them a dish for water or get a special bottle from the pet store. Wild gerbils living in the desert make their homes in tunnels that they dig with their strong claws. Their instinct to dig is very strong, so they might even try to dig in a plastic, wooden, metal, or glass cage. In the wild, they make nests out of grass, leaves, and seeds, but as pets, they like to shred clean washcloths or empty bathroom tissue rolls into small pieces to make their nests.

 In the wild

 Applying knowledge
"We found out that wild gerbils live in the desert. How do you think being able to jump and leap helps them? Does it help them get away from predators like snakes and foxes? Does it keep their feet from getting too hot?"

Food pellets for gerbils can be bought at a pet store. You can give gerbils a little lettuce, carrot, cabbage, or celery several times a week, but be careful; too much fresh food might make them sick.

Gerbils are usually easy to tame. They are not as nervous as mice. They do not run and hide as quickly as mice. They can squeeze into small places like hamsters do.

One way to pick up a gerbil is to put your hand inside the cage and see if the gerbil will crawl onto your hand. Then you can lift it out. Another way is to grasp it by the base of the tail. Slowly lift it out of the cage with its head down. Then you can lower it into your hand. Never lift a gerbil by the end of its tail!

A pet gerbil lives for about four years.

Let's Create a Gerbil Care Can

Increasing observational techniques by creating a model of a gerbil; manipulating materials; following directions; measuring with a tape, a ruler, and possibly a compass; learning about geometrical shapes; using reference material to learn what an animal needs for life

Create your Gerbil Care Can from a cylinder such as a coffee can or an oatmeal box (Fig. 3-8). Fill it with things that help you take care of your pet, such as food, vitamins, chew sticks, and nesting material.

■ **3-8** *A Gerbil Care Can.*

What you need

- [ ] Book about taking care of gerbils and other small pets
- [ ] Empty cylinder with a lid such as a coffee can or an oatmeal box
- [ ] Tape measure
- [ ] Ruler
- [ ] Drawing compass (optional)
- [ ] Pencil
- [ ] Construction paper
- [ ] Scissors
- [ ] Paper punch
- [ ] Glue
- [ ] Markers

A note to the adult Use this activity to teach beginning concepts in measuring. To turn each container into a gerbil, it must first be covered with paper. Show your students how to use a tape measure and a ruler to discover the circumference and the height of their containers. Then help them draw and cut out a rectangle with these dimensions.

They must also cover the lid of the container. Help them trace around the lid directly onto the paper they will use for covering it, or show them how to copy the dimensions of the lid by using a compass.

To speed up the project, cut the construction paper beforehand. Just remember: the more work you do for them, the less students learn to do for themselves.

Directions

1. Remove the lid of the can. Use the tape measure to find the circumference of the can. Write the measurement on a piece of scrap paper. Add 1 inch to the measurement so you can overlap and glue your paper as you construct the care can.

2. Use the ruler to measure the height of the can. Write down that measurement also. Now use the ruler to draw a rectangle on construction paper using these dimensions.

3. Cut out the rectangle. Spread glue on one side of it and wrap the rectangle around the can with the glue side against the can.

4. Trace around the lid onto construction paper or use a drawing compass to copy the dimensions of the lid onto paper. Cut out the resulting circle and glue it on top of the lid.

5. Use the patterns in Fig. 3-9 to trace and cut out the nose, tail, back legs, front legs, ears, and eyes.

6. To form the nose into a cone shape, begin by holding the nose cutout with the flat edge at the top. Holding it at each point, pull your hands together and downward. Overlap the edges until the paper comes to a sharp point at the top. (It should look like a tepee.) Glue the cone to make it hold its shape.

7. To glue the nose onto the gerbil, first draw three ½-inch slits straight up from the base of the cone; space them equally apart. Cut the slits and spread them apart to make three tabs. Put glue on the tabs. Glue the

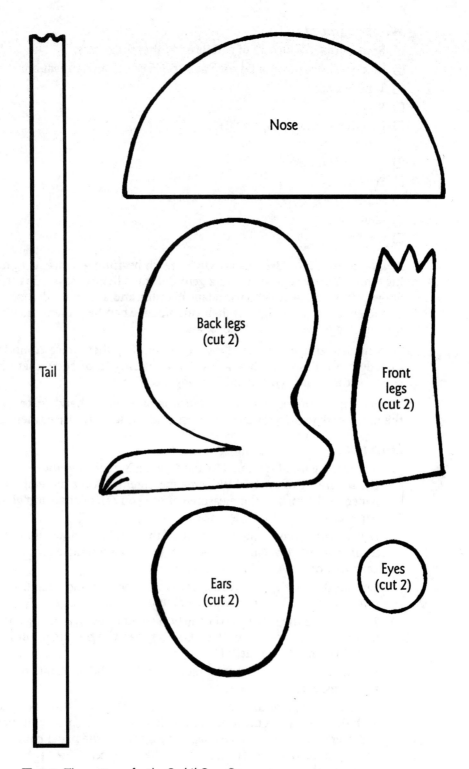

■ **3-9** *The patterns for the Gerbil Care Can.*

nose onto the can. Add a paper-punch circle to its tip. Make two teeth out of white paper and glue them under the nose.

8. Glue the tail to the back of the gerbil. Glue the eyes just above the nose and add paper-punch eyeballs. Glue on the front legs, the back legs, and the ears. Use a marker to add eyelashes and tiny claws.

Pet pause *Pet gerbils are descendants of 20 pairs of gerbils taken from Mongolia in 1935. The gerbils were sent to Tokyo for breeding in a laboratory. In 1954, 22 of these gerbils (11 pairs) were sent to the United States for scientific research. They were bred, and, within 10 years, there were thousands of Mongolian gerbils in this country. The scientists who worked with them learned that they are very gentle, and soon gerbils became popular pets.*

Gerbils are useful laboratory animals. Researchers use them to study various diseases and the effects of space flight.

☞ Let's be nocturnal

Designing investigations

Since the pets we have studied in this chapter are nocturnal, let the children experience dim light activities. Tell the children that you are going to turn off the lights for 10 minutes. Have them work, play, or just move about quietly without the overhead lighting. If you have windows, you should have a little natural light. If you have no windows, turn on a small lamp, so that the general lighting for the room will be dim. Ask the children to lie down and pretend to be asleep while the lights are on. When the room gets dark, have them quietly move about to play, read, write, or do an assigned activity selected by you. After the experience, talk with the children about how they felt and what they were thinking. You might want to let the children design other investigations in which they try out the attributes of rodents.

☞ Favorite food

Making predictions

From the pet store, get food that has a variety of seeds and pellets in it. Put a small amount in the pet's dish. Watch carefully to see which item it picks up first. Is this its favorite food? The next time you feed it, prepare a tray with the types of food clearly separated. If you can get a large box, put the pet and the tray in it. Predict which food item the pet might go to first. Does it go to the nearest food, or does it go to the food you think is its favorite? Finding out should be fun.

☞ Make a maze

Designing investigations

If you have large wooden blocks, let the children create a maze on the floor with food at the end of it. You could also create a maze with small blocks or Legos in the pet's cage. (Take everything else out of the cage while you do this investigation.) Let the pet go through the maze several times. Does it go the same way each time? Encourage the children to watch carefully or have someone videotape this experiment. Discuss what happens.

☞ *Closure*

🔍 *Applying knowledge; drawing conclusions*

Bringing closure to your study is important. Review your initial goals, and let the children talk about what they have learned and how they are using what they have learned. The following are some ideas to help bring closure to your study:

1. Let the children write a cinquain about a mouse, hamster, or gerbil. A cinquain is composed of five lines.
   - One word for the title
   - Two words to describe the title
   - Three words to express action
   - Four words to express feeling
   - The title again

2. Make a chart to help you discuss how mice, hamsters, and gerbils are alike and how they are different. For example, your chart might look like the following:

**How Mice, Hamsters,
and Gerbils Are Alike**
They have four legs.
They are active at night.

**Mice, Hamsters,
and Gerbils Are Different**
Only a hamster has pouches.
Mice and gerbils have long tails;
hamsters have short tails.

RABBITS & GUINEA PIGS

Science goals

To help children become aware of what these animals are like, how they behave as pets, and how we can take care of them

Teacher/Parent planning

Think about how you can get a rabbit or guinea pig to the class for a visit. Send a letter home asking parents to bring the animal to school for a visit. Borrow informational books from the library. Prepare to write words about the particular animal on a large sheet of chart paper.

Materials needed for discussion and activities

- ☐ Live animals for observation
- ☐ Informational books from the library
- ☐ *The Tale of Peter Rabbit*
- ☐ Fruits and vegetables
- ☐ Video camera and equipment
- ☐ Poster materials

Related words

mammal An animal that has hair or fur, is warm-blooded, whose young are born alive and drink milk from their mother, and breathes with lungs

herbivore An animal that eats only plants

Rabbits

Rabbits are interesting animals known for hopping, wiggling their noses, and being soft to pet. Rabbits are mammals, which means they have fur, are warm-blooded, breathe with lungs, and drink milk from their mothers when they are young. Rabbits have long ears and a short, fluffy tail. You can buy a rabbit at a pet store or get one from someone who has a rabbit to sell or give away.

☞ *A visit with a rabbit*

🔍 *Observing*

Let your children observe a rabbit in a cage or while its owner holds it. Talk about and point out the following:

- ☐ Fur (Talk about the color and texture.)
- ☐ Long, silky ears, which move in every direction to pick up sounds
- ☐ Eyes on the sides of the head
- ☐ Eyebrows, which are used for feeling
- ☐ Nose (Rabbits have a keen sense of smell.)
- ☐ Delicate whiskers, which sense danger
- ☐ Mouth, with as many as 28 teeth
- ☐ Two chisel-like teeth for gnawing
- ☐ Front feet (Sharp nails are for burrowing in soil.)

□ Hind feet, used for thumping to communicate with each other and for self-defense. (Nails are used for scratching and grooming itself.)

□ Small, fluffy tail

The fur of pet rabbits can be brown, black, white, gray, or combinations of these colors. Some rabbits have short fur, and others have long fur that has to be brushed each day. Most rabbits have ears that stand up, but some rabbits have floppy ears that touch the ground.

 Ears

 Drawing conclusions

Talk with the children about their own ears, and how their ears are shaped to capture sound waves. If their ears are covered, they cannot hear as well.

"Rabbits with floppy ears cannot hear as well as rabbits with upright ears. Why do you think this is true?"

Pet rabbits can grow to be 10 to 20 inches long and weigh from 3 to 10 pounds. A rabbit's tail is about 2 inches long and is covered with soft, fluffy fur that makes it look round.

> ***Pet pause*** *A male rabbit is called a buck, the female is called a doe, and the young are called kittens.*

Wild rabbits might live in a shallow hole covered by shrubs, weeds, grass, or leaves. They can also live in underground rooms called burrows, which are usually dug by the female rabbits or by other animals like woodchucks. Rabbits in the wild eat and play during the day and rest and sleep at night. Rabbits eat grass, clover, and weeds in spring and summer. In the winter, they eat twigs and any fruit that they can find. Rabbits get into people's gardens and nibble on beans, lettuce, or other vegetables.

 The Tale of Peter Rabbit

Classifying

Plan a time to read this book and also watch the video if you can get it through a movie rental store. Also, try to find information about Beatrix Potter. She carefully observed rabbits to help her draw realistic illustrations of rabbits. She loved to watch animals.

After enjoying the book, talk about the parts of the story that could be real and the parts that are make-believe. You might make a list like the following:

Real	Make-believe
Peter had a mother and siblings.	Rabbits talk.
Rabbits live under the ground.	Rabbits have furniture.
Rabbits go into gardens.	Rabbits wear clothes.
Rabbits like lettuce and beans.	Rabbits drink tea.
Rabbits can get frightened.	
People chase rabbits.	
Rabbits get sick from eating too much.	

Let's Create Peter Rabbit's Jacket and Ears

 Learning to measure and draw with a ruler; manipulating materials; following directions

Peter Rabbit's Jacket

First create a jacket to wear to Peter Rabbit's party (Fig. 4-1). Start with a large grocery bag. Snip it and decorate it to be the best-dressed rabbit there!

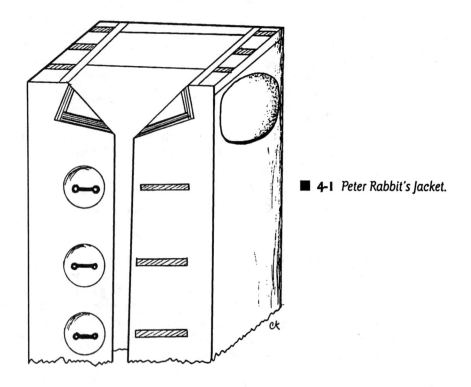

■ **4-1** *Peter Rabbit's Jacket.*

What you need
- ☐ Large, paper, flat-bottom grocery bag
- ☐ Scissors
- ☐ Ruler
- ☐ Construction paper
- ☐ White glue
- ☐ Markers
- ☐ Tape to repair torn jacket

Directions to make Peter Rabbit's Jacket

1. Cut the bottom of the bag up the middle, from the opening to the bag bottom as shown in Fig. 4-2.
2. Cut out the bag bottom, leaving a 3-inch piece on each side to form shoulders for the jacket as shown in Fig. 4-3. Use the ruler to measure these shoulders.

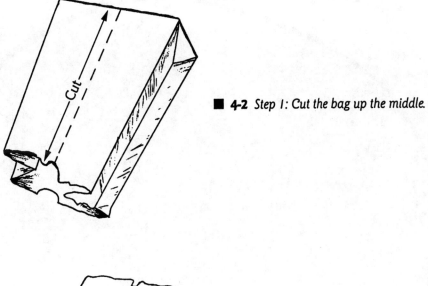

■ **4-2** *Step 1: Cut the bag up the middle.*

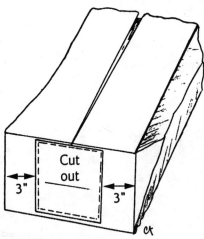

■ **4-3** *Step 2: Cut out the bag bottom, leaving 3-inch shoulders.*

3. Use the armhole pattern (Fig. 4-4) to trace and cut out an armhole on each side of the bag as shown in Fig. 4-5.
4. Fold down the front edges to create lapels, shown in Fig. 4-6.
5. Use the patterns in Fig. 4-7 to trace buttons and buttonholes onto construction paper. Cut these out and glue them on your jacket.
6. Use the tail pattern in Fig. 4-7 to cut out a construction paper tail. Glue wisps of cotton onto it. Don't add too much cotton or it will be too heavy! Glue the tail onto the back of your jacket.
7. If you like, add other decorations with construction paper, glue, and markers.

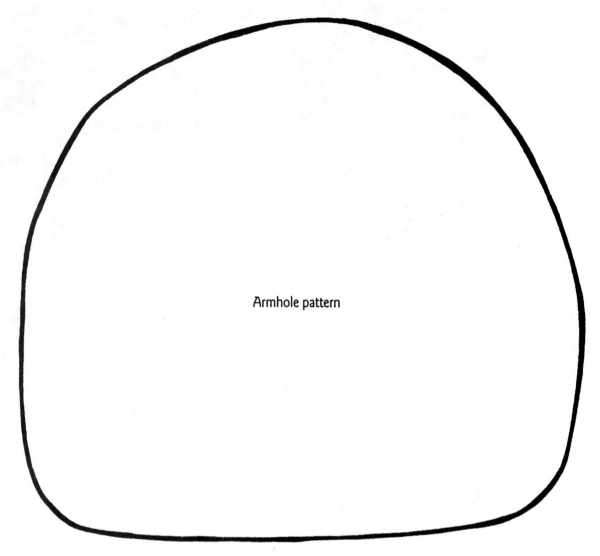

Armhole pattern

■ **4-4** *The pattern for the armholes in Peter Rabbit's Jacket.*

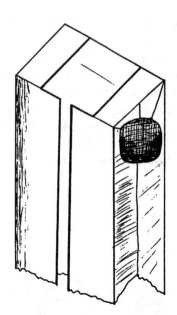

■ **4-5** *Step 3: Cut out an armhole on each side of the bag.*

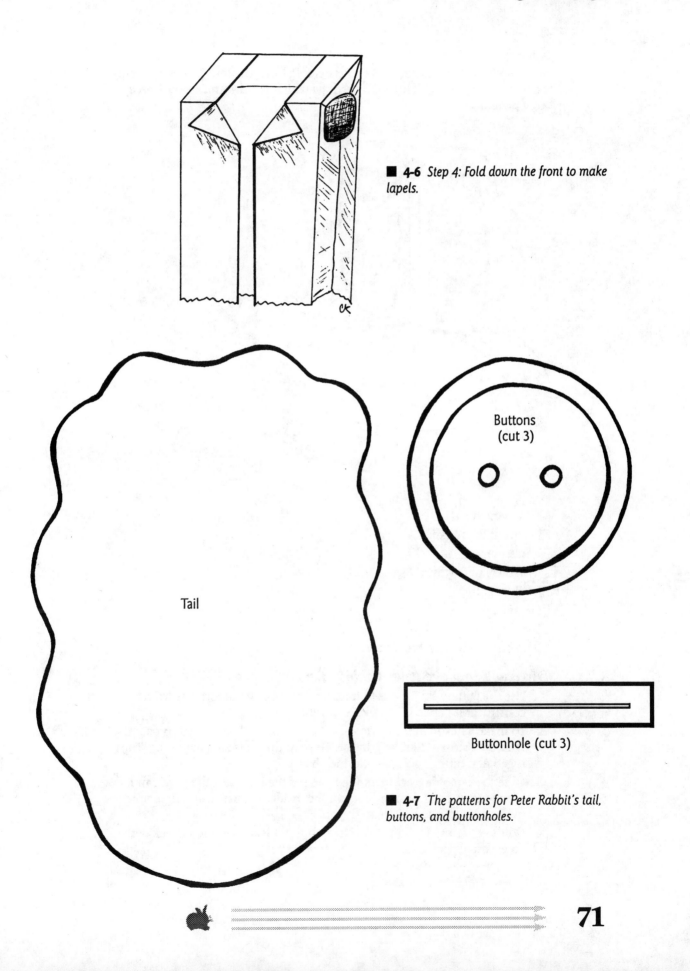

■ **4-6** *Step 4: Fold down the front to make lapels.*

Buttons
(cut 3)

Tail

Buttonhole (cut 3)

■ **4-7** *The patterns for Peter Rabbit's tail, buttons, and buttonholes.*

Peter Rabbit's Ears
Now make long ears to complete your Peter Rabbit costume (Fig. 4-8). Color the tip of your nose with lipstick and draw whiskers on your face with an eyebrow pencil!

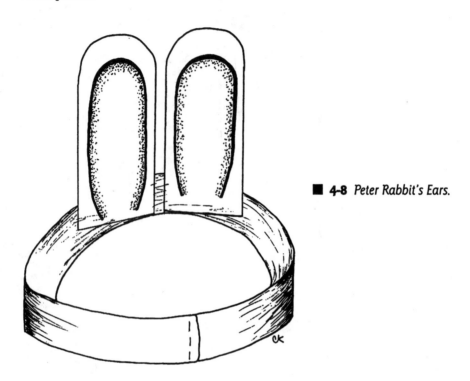

■ *4-8 Peter Rabbit's Ears.*

What you need
☐ Construction paper
☐ Scissors
☐ Markers or crayons
☐ White glue
☐ Stapler
☐ Red lipstick
☐ Brown or black eyebrow pencil

Directions to make Peter Rabbit's Ears

1. Use the pattern in Fig. 4-9 to trace and cut out two rabbit ears from construction paper. If you like, color the ears.
2. To make a headband, cut two 4-x-12-inch strips of construction paper. Fold each strip in half lengthwise. Overlap the ends and staple the strips together creating a long 2-x-20-inch band.
3. Glue the ears side by side on the inside of the band. Fit the headband around your head with the ears on the inside, against your hair. Staple the headband into a circle to fit you.
4. Color your nose with lipstick. Draw three whiskers on each cheek with an eyebrow pencil.

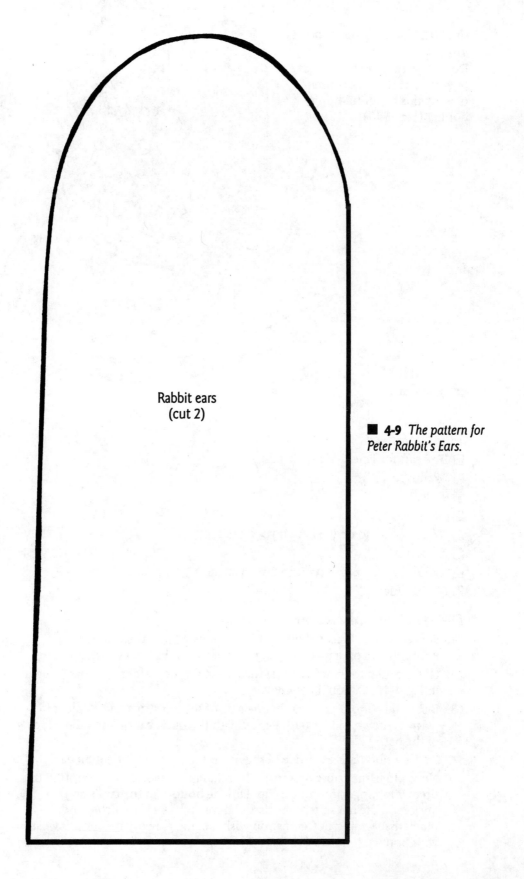

Rabbit ears
(cut 2)

■ **4-9** *The pattern for Peter Rabbit's Ears.*

Bonnets for Flopsie, Mopsie, and Cottontail

Do you want to go to the party as one of Peter Rabbit's sisters? Try making this beautiful bunny bonnet (Fig. 4-10).

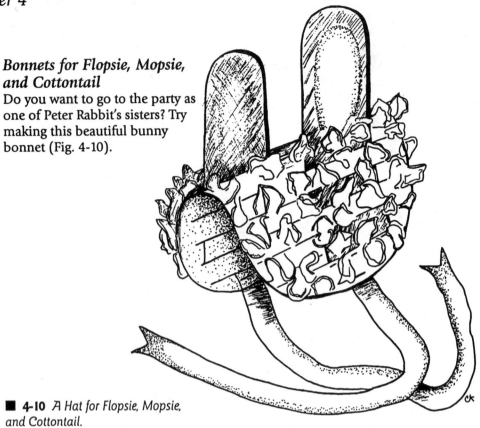

■ **4-10** *A Hat for Flopsie, Mopsie, and Cottontail.*

What you need
- [ ] The ears for Peter Rabbit's headband
- [ ] Wallpaper
- [ ] Ruler
- [ ] Scissors
- [ ] Wide ribbon to tie the hat on your head
- [ ] Stapler
- [ ] Colored tissue paper cut into 2-inch squares
- [ ] White glue

Directions to make a Bonnet

1. First create the Peter Rabbit Ears. Then draw a "watermelon shape" 9 × 12 inches on a piece of wallpaper as shown in Fig. 4-11. Cut it out.
2. Use the ruler to draw lines one inch apart on the watermelon hat, shown in Fig. 4-12. Cut on these lines.
3. Insert the bottom of an ear in one side of the hat strips and staple it in place as shown in Fig. 4-13. Repeat with the other ear on the other side of the hat.
4. Staple a ribbon to each side of the hat at the base of each rabbit ear.
5. Now add tissue paper flowers to the hat. Press a tissue square around the tip of your finger, forming a cup. Dip the bottom of the cup into glue. Stick it on the hat so that the tissue sticks up like a little flower. Add as many tissue paper flowers as you wish. Let the glue dry before you wear your bonnet.

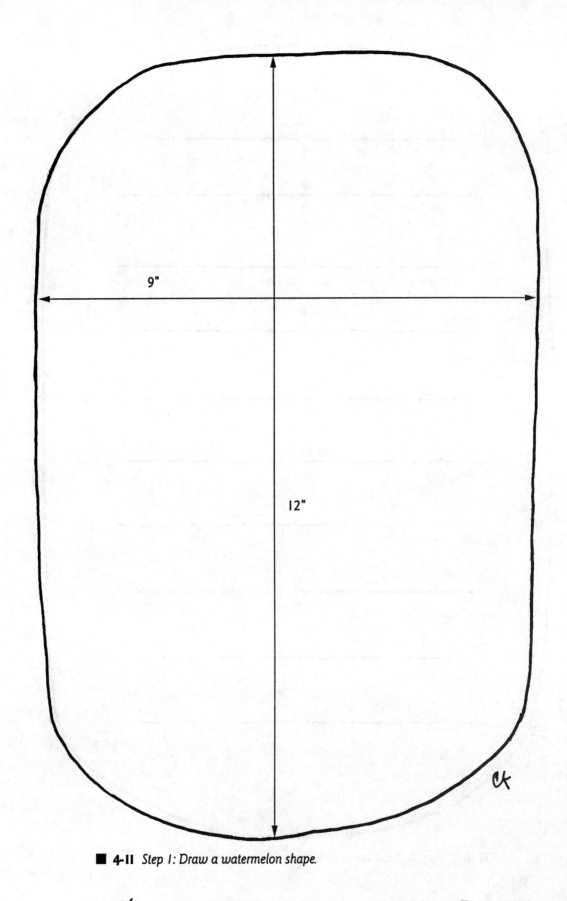

9"

12"

■ **4-11** *Step 1: Draw a watermelon shape.*

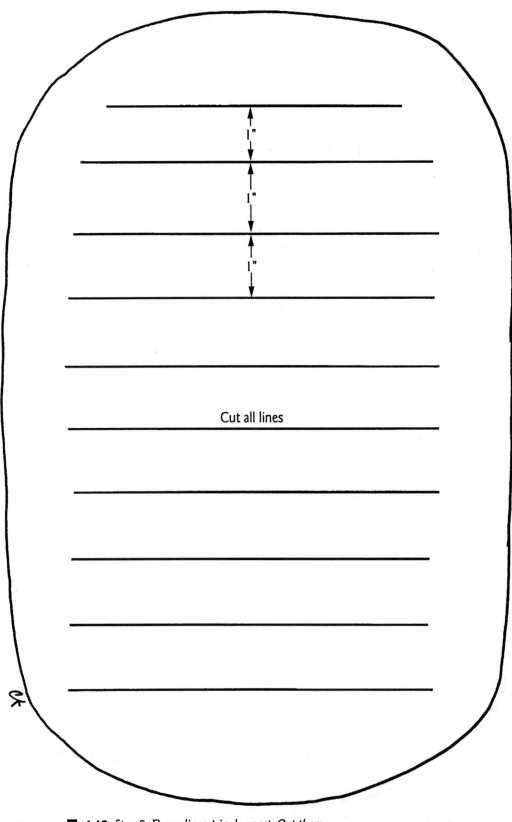

Cut all lines

1"

1"

1"

■ **4-12** *Step 2: Draw lines 1 inch apart. Cut them.*

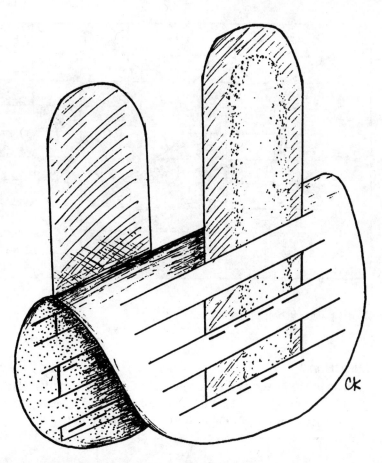

■ **4-13** *Step 3: Insert the bottom of the ears through the strips.*

Let's Create Peter Rabbit's Place Mat

 Learning to measure and draw with a ruler; manipulating materials; following directions
Design a place mat for Peter Rabbit's party (Fig. 4-14). Cover it with clear contact paper or with a plastic kitchen bag so it can be kept clean with a damp cloth.

What you need
☐ 9-×-12-inch red and purple construction paper
☐ Ruler
☐ Pencil
☐ Scissors
☐ White glue
☐ Markers
☐ Clear contact paper or a 11½-×-12½-inch plastic kitchen bag
☐ Orange and green construction paper

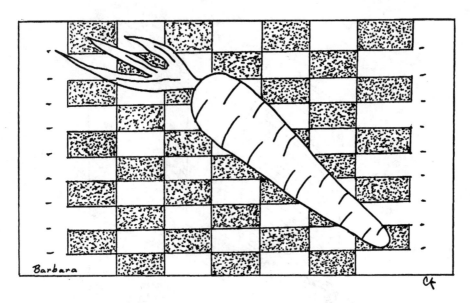

■ **4-14** Peter Rabbit's placemat.

Directions

1. Lay the ruler across the narrow end of the purple paper. Use the pencil to draw eight dots at 1-inch intervals (Fig. 4-15). Move the ruler down several inches. Draw eight more dots 1 inch apart.

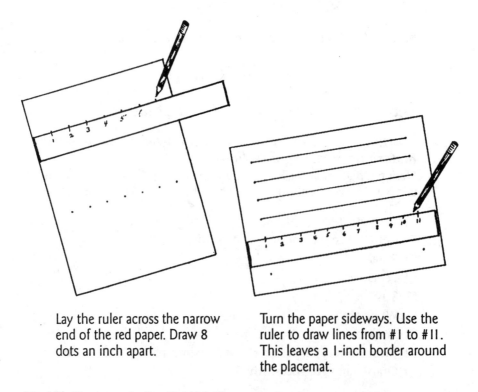

Lay the ruler across the narrow end of the red paper. Draw 8 dots an inch apart.

Turn the paper sideways. Use the ruler to draw lines from #1 to #11. This leaves a 1-inch border around the placemat.

■ **4-15** *How to make Peter Rabbit's Placemat.*

2. Turn the paper sideways. Lay the ruler across the page. Use the dots to draw a straight line from the 1-inch mark to 11-inch mark on the ruler (Fig. 4-15). Make eight of these lines. Use scissors to cut on these lines, leaving a 1-inch border around the edges of the place mat.

3. Use the ruler to measure ten 1-x-12-inch red strips. Cut them out. Weave the red strips in and out of the purple place mat. Push the woven strips as close together as you can while you work.

4. Trim the red strips so the ends are even with the purple place mat. Put a dot of glue under the ends to hold them.

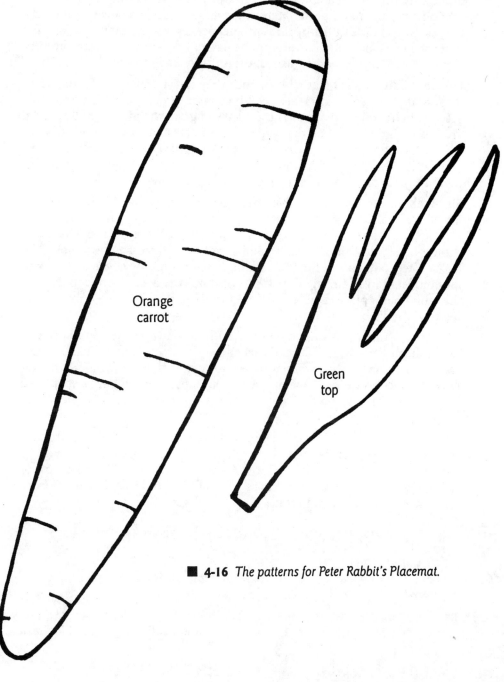

Orange carrot

Green top

■ **4-16** *The patterns for Peter Rabbit's Placemat.*

5. Use the pattern in Fig. 4-16 to trace an orange carrot and a green top. Cut them out and glue them on the place mat.

6. Cover the place mat with clear contact paper, or slide it into a plastic kitchen bag and tape it underneath to make a mat that can be wiped clean after use.

 A Peter Rabbit party

 Observing

Plan a Peter Rabbit party at which the children eat rabbit food. Send notes home with the children asking them to bring one of the following foods to school: carrots, lettuce, parsley, tender green beans, English peas, and blackberries. (If you have difficulty finding blackberries, you might try looking for them at a local farmer's market or in the frozen freezer section of the grocery store.) The foods should be washed, cut up, and ready to eat.

Let the children dress up as rabbits. Then they can sit in a circle on the floor. Prior to the party, you can let the children color or paint a garden on a long piece of bulletin board paper. The garden can go in the middle of the circle. They can put their food on the place mats they created. Pass out one food at a time. Talk about how each one looks, smells, feels, tastes, and sounds when you eat it. Save the blackberries for dessert. You can eat them plain or dip them in white sugar, brown sugar, or whipped topping.

Since rabbits are large and active, they need plenty of space. Rabbits need a large home called a hutch. A hutch is a large wooden cage. If it is kept outside, it should have four tall legs that keep it high off the ground. The hutch should be about 4 or 5 feet long and 2 or 3 feet deep. The legs should be about 3 feet tall. Part of the front of the hutch should be covered with wire mesh to let in fresh air, and the other part should be a solid wooden door so the rabbit has a place to hide and be warm. Hutches need two rooms: a living room and a bedroom.

The floor of the hutch should be lined with paper. Over the paper, you put wood shavings and straw for bedding and some hay for eating. Rabbit food can be purchased at a pet store. You need to get heavy bowls for food and water, or a water bottle, from the pet store. Your rabbit should have a small tree branch on which to gnaw. Gnawing keeps the rabbit's teeth healthy and keeps the teeth from growing too long.

A rabbit can be kept indoors. The rabbit can be trained to go to the bathroom in a litter tray, much like one for a cat. The rabbit needs a special cage in which to sleep. If the rabbit is indoors, it needs to stay out of its cage most of the day so it can get enough exercise. The rabbit should be kept away from any other pets that might hurt it.

 Harmful or not harmful

 Asking questions

"What kinds of pets might hurt a rabbit? What kinds of pets might not hurt a rabbit?"

Rabbits are herbivores, which means they only eat plants. They like grass and clover. They like fresh fruits like apple, pear, and cantaloupe. They like fresh vegetables like celery, cabbage, turnip, lettuce, spinach, carrot, cucumber, and cauliflower. Rabbits need a variety of these foods each day. Instead of walking or running like most four-legged animals, rabbits hop. Their hind legs are longer and stronger than their front legs, so the hind legs do much of the work in hopping, but rabbits use their front legs to balance themselves as they hop.

☞ *Hopping like a rabbit*

Creating models

Have the children to squat down. Tell them to hop forward, using their hands to help them balance as they land on the floor. (Their hands may remain in the air or land palms down on the floor.) Let the children do this several times, then discuss this type of movement.

Rabbits need to visit a veterinarian once a year for a checkup and every six months for inoculations or shots to keep it from getting bad diseases. A healthy pet rabbit can live for about five years.

Guinea pigs

Guinea pigs are not really pigs. They are small, furry animals that originally came from South America. They are a type of mammal, which means they have fur or hair, are warm-blooded, breathe with lungs, and drink milk from their mothers when they are young. Guinea pigs are rodents. A rodent is an animal with special front teeth adapted for gnawing and nibbling. These teeth grow throughout the animal's life, so they must constantly be worn away by gnawing on something hard. Some other types of rodents are mice, hamsters, gerbils, beavers, chipmunks, and squirrels. Guinea pigs are *diurnal*, which means that they sleep at night and are active during the day.

No one knows for sure how guinea pigs got their name. Some people think their squeaking sound is like that of a pig. Perhaps sailors who brought them out of South America sailed from Guiana. Some people call guinea pigs by their scientific name, which is *cavy*. In the wild, cavies make their homes in the mountains (where they live in burrows or in nests among rocks) and grasslands (where they make nests in the tall grasses) of South America.

In the wild, guinea pigs are likely to be caught by larger animals, so they are very shy and easily frightened. They cannot move as quickly as mice, so their natural instinct is to hide when they get frightened. As pets, they always need a quiet place where they can go to feel safe.

☞ *A visit with a guinea pig*

Observing

Arrange for someone to bring a guinea pig and its cage. Let the owner hold it and tell the children about it; then, let the children observe it in its cage. Talk about the following:

☐ Fur (color, texture)

☐ Ears (They have excellent hearing.)

☐ Nose (They have a good sense of smell.)

☐ Eyes (big, bright)
☐ Whiskers
☐ Mouth and teeth
☐ Paws (The front paws have four toes and the back paws have three toes.)

Let the children hold the guinea pig if you and its owner feel it is safe. They hardly ever bite, but all precautions should be taken. The proper way to hold it is to slide one hand under its body, then place the other hand on top of the guinea pig to lift it carefully up. You should always support the guinea pig; its bones are very fragile. Remind the children to be quiet and gentle.

You can buy a guinea pig at a pet store or get one from someone you know who wants to sell or give one away. An adult guinea pig is about 10 to 14 inches long and weighs about 2 pounds. Baby guinea pigs are fully developed when they are born. While baby hamsters and mice have no hair, cannot see, and are very helpless, baby guinea pigs have plenty of hair and can see well. They are very active only 30 minutes after they are born. They might even start to clean themselves at that time. After only two days, they begin to eat the same food their mother eats, but they continue to drink milk from her for two or three weeks.

Guinea pigs come in different colors and have different kinds of hair. Smooth-haired guinea pigs have short, smooth hair. Rough-haired guinea pigs have long, coarse hair. Long-haired guinea pigs need extra grooming to keep their hair from getting tangled. If we say a guinea pig is self-colored that means it is the same color all over. This color can be black, white, red, brown, beige, golden, or lilac. Some guinea pigs are speckled, which means there are different colors on each strand of hair. Some guinea pigs have a pattern of colors on their bodies.

☞ *Research*

Finding information
Give the children time to look through informational books to find pictures of guinea pigs. Talk about the pictures.

Let's Create a Model Guinea Pig

Learning about the anatomy of a guinea pig by drawing a model; using reference material to find out about and create a suitable home for this popular pet
A guinea pig has a small, stout body, short ears, and almost no tail at all. Draw or construct a pet guinea pig. Then create a place for him to live.

What you need
☐ Book about guinea pigs
☐ Construction paper or drawing paper
☐ Pencil
☐ Crayons
☐ Scissors
☐ White glue

Directions

1. Find out what guinea pigs look like by observing live ones and then by reading about them in books.
2. Use the pattern in Fig. 4-17 to draw an egg-shaped body to make the guinea pig model and cut it out.
3. Add ears, nose, eyes, legs, fur, and other parts either by drawing and coloring, or by cutting construction paper and gluing it to the body.
4. Draw or construct a place for your guinea pig to live. Make sure it has proper food, clean water, and a comfortable bed.

As pets, guinea pigs should live in a hutch, which is a large wooden cage. It should have two rooms. One room should be closed off by wood on all sides, but it should have an opening into the other room. The other room should have wire mesh on one or more sides. The hutch could stand on tall legs so that dogs or cats can't get to it. You can keep the hutch inside or outside, but keep it out of bad weather and in a very safe place. Guinea pigs can get sick if they get too cold or wet.

Guinea pigs like clean hay. They eat it, sleep in it, and play with it. They also need clean wood shavings in their hutch. You should be careful not to ever

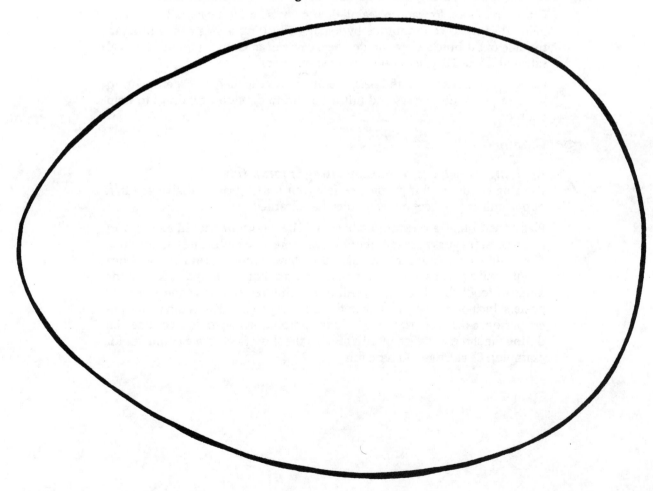

■ **4-17** *Let's Create a Guinea Pig*

get hay or shavings that have been exposed to harmful chemicals. Guinea pigs like to be very clean, so their cage should be cleaned out every few days. They are even careful to go to the bathroom in only one corner of their cage. They try to keep their home very clean.

 Cleaning

Applying knowledge

Plan a special time to clean the classroom. Talk about the importance of keeping our work and play areas clean. Give each child a specific job to do. After the cleaning time, talk about how the room looks and how much better we feel in a nicely cleaned environment. Talk about how pets depend on us to keep their homes clean and healthy for them.

You need a heavy bowl for food and a special water bottle from the pet store. The water bottle should be made of glass; guinea pigs can chew plastic ones. You need something in the cage for the guinea pig to gnaw on, like a piece of wood.

Guinea pigs need to be fed once each day. They are herbivores; they like hay, grain, vegetables like cabbage, cauliflower leaves, lettuce, carrot tops, celery, and fruits like apple. You can buy special dry food at the pet store.

Guinea pigs look forward to seeing their owners and to being talked to and held. They try to communicate by making whistling noises and coming to the side of the hutch when their owners come near. Guinea pigs need to feel safe and loved. They live about five to seven years.

Guinea pigs make wonderful pets. Scientists also use them in experiments to learn more about diseases and nutrition and to develop new drugs to help people.

 Closure

Applying knowledge; communicating information

To bring closure to this chapter, review your initial goals and give children opportunities to talk about what they have learned.

Plan to videotape a classroom talk show. The talk show should have a host and a guest (or guests) to talk about how to care for a rabbit and a guinea pig. The children can use play animals they have brought from home. They should make posters to show how the animals' homes should look and the kinds of foods they need to eat. All of the children can draw and color the posters. Include as many people in the show as you can. You can have a camera person, a director, people to hold the posters, people to do a commercial during the show, and even more guests on the show (a pet store employee for example). Be creative and have fun.

BIRDS

Science goals

To help children become aware of what birds are like, how they behave as
pets, and how we can take care of them

Teacher/Parent planning

Think about how you can get a bird to the class for a visit. Send a note home
to secure a parent volunteer. You might plan a field trip to a pet shop. Borrow
informational books from the library. Prepare to write words or sentences on a
large sheet of chart paper. Ask children to bring in any pictures of birds they have.

Materials needed for discussion and activities

☐ Live birds for observation
☐ Informational books
☐ Storybooks
☐ Camera
☐ Watercolor paints, brushes, and paper

Related words

vertebrate An animal with a backbone

feathers Structures that cover a bird's skin

Birds have three kinds of feathers: flight feathers, which are in their wings
and tails to help them fly; downy feathers, which are small and soft to keep
them warm; and body feathers, which cover the rest of the bird's body.

Birds belong to a group of animals called vertebrates, which means that they
have backbones. Birds are warm-blooded, which means their body temperature always remains about the same regardless of the temperature of their
surroundings. Baby birds hatch from eggs. Birds' bodies are covered with
feathers. Birds do not have teeth. They have beaks, which are used for self-defense and for getting food. Nearly all birds have a voice and they use it to call
or sing.

Visiting with a bird

Observing

Arrange for a bird to be brought into class for a visit. The bird should remain
in its cage while the children observe it. Guide the children as they look and
listen. Help them notice and talk about the following:

☐ Head (eyes, beak with nostrils)
☐ Feathers (color, length)
☐ Feet
☐ Tail
☐ Size of the bird
☐ Noises it makes

Birds can see very well. Most birds' eyes are on the sides of their heads and
each eye sees something different. (Our eyes are on the front of our faces and

both eyes see the same thing. As for birds, an owl is an example of a bird whose eyes are on the front.)

Birds have an ear on each side of their head. They have an outer ear (covered with feathers) and an inner ear. They can hear well.

Birds do not depend much on their senses of smell, taste, and touch.

Birds breathe in air through their mouth and nostrils (two holes in their beak) to their lungs. Some of the air travels to air sacs between different parts of their bodies. This air cools the inside of the bird.

Birds do not have teeth, so they cannot chew their food. They have to cut it up with their beaks or swallow it whole.

Birds have a heart, a brain, and many other organs in its body just like we do.

Birds have feathers. They care for their feathers by cleaning them with their beak. This process is called *preening*. A preen gland at the base of the tail produces oil. Birds use their beaks to make the oil come out of the preen gland and to put the oil on their feathers. The oil keeps the feathers waterproof and pretty.

 A visit to a pet shop

Observing; asking questions; finding information

Pet shops have a wonderful variety of birds. Plan to visit and take a guided tour. Bring a camera and take pictures of the different types of birds. You can use the pictures later when you discuss the birds and complete other activities.

A bird needs a large cage. The bottom of the cage should be lined with newspaper and perhaps wood shavings. The bird needs to stand and sleep on a perch placed in the cage. You can use a stick from a tree or buy a perch from the pet store. The bird needs water and the proper type of food, which you also buy from the pet store. A bird needs some fresh food, also. Fresh foods might include carrots, spinach, peas, celery, parsley, apple, or pear. A bird needs calcium. Put clean eggshells or a cuttle bone in the cage to give the bird calcium. Gnawing helps keep the beak from getting too long. A bird needs something wooden on which to gnaw.

Pet birds need exercise to stay healthy. They should be allowed to fly around a room for about 20 minutes a day. Be sure that all windows are closed and there are no openings, like a fireplace, where the bird might get out. If you want to catch the bird, turn the lights off to calm it and throw a large, soft cloth over it. Then gently lift up the bird.

When your bird sleeps at night, cover the cage with a large sheet or other cloth. The bird sleeps comfortably in this darkened environment.

People have been keeping birds as pets for many years. Favorite bird pets include canaries, parakeets, parrots, cockatiels, and finches.

Canaries are usually bright yellow in color. They are known for their songs and their cheerfulness. They originally came from the Canary Islands.

Parakeets are members of the parrot family. Parakeets are brightly colored. They can be green, red, blue, orange, yellow, pink, and purple. Parakeets have cone-shaped beaks. This kind of beak helps them crack and pick up seeds. Parakeets are smart. They can be trained to talk. If you say the same word or phrase over and over, the bird might learn to say it, also. A parakeet might learn to say its own name. Parakeets live about five years.

Parrots are large, colorful birds. In the wild, they are found in warm, tropical parts of the world. They can be very loving and can learn to talk. They can grow to be about 3 feet tall. Parrots have thick, curved beaks. The sharp point and hooked shape of the beak help them pierce and eat fruits. The beak allows the parrot to crack nuts or seeds.

Cockatiels are members of the parrot family. Their coloring can be gray, white, black, red, rose, and yellow. They have a crest on their head. The *crest* is a tuft of feathers that stands up above the head. Cockatiels have curved beaks. They can live about 15 years.

Finches are seedeaters. Their beaks are cone-shaped, so they can stab into seeds. Many finches are gray or brown, but their beaks are a more colorful orange or red. Their feet can be orange also. Finches like company, so keeping more than one together in a large cage is good.

Many pet birds are very social. They become attached to the members of their family, and they do not like strangers. They communicate with their family members by chirping, squawking, bobbing their heads, and climbing on the side of the cage. They show pleasure or displeasure through their actions and sounds.

The larger the type of bird, the longer its life span is. Small birds such as parakeets live about 5 years, and large birds such as parrots live about 60 or 70 years.

Pet pause An expert on birds is called an ornithologist.

☞ *Watercolor painting*

 Finding information; recording information
Let children look through the photographs from the pet shop and through informational books. Let them choose a bird to paint with watercolors onto white construction paper. (Use a simple watercolor tray and brush.) Display the paintings.

Let's Create a Paper Plate Cockatiel

 Becoming familiar with the anatomy of a bird by creating a model; manipulating materials; using reference material
A paper plate is just the right shape to create a pet cockatiel or finch (Fig. 5-1). Choose the body that you want to trace. With the help of a string, your bird can flap its wings!

What you need
☐ Books about real pet birds
☐ 9-inch white paper plate
☐ Pencil
☐ Scissors

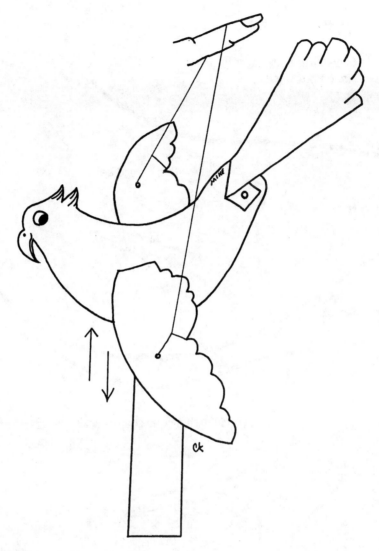

■ **5-1** *The Paper Plate Cockatiel.*

☐ Crayons
☐ Markers
☐ White glue
☐ Stapler
☐ Paper fastener
☐ 20-inch piece of string
☐ Cardboard to make a handle

Directions

1. In the media center or library, find some books about pet birds. As you create your bird, try to make it look like a real cockatiel, finch, or parakeet.

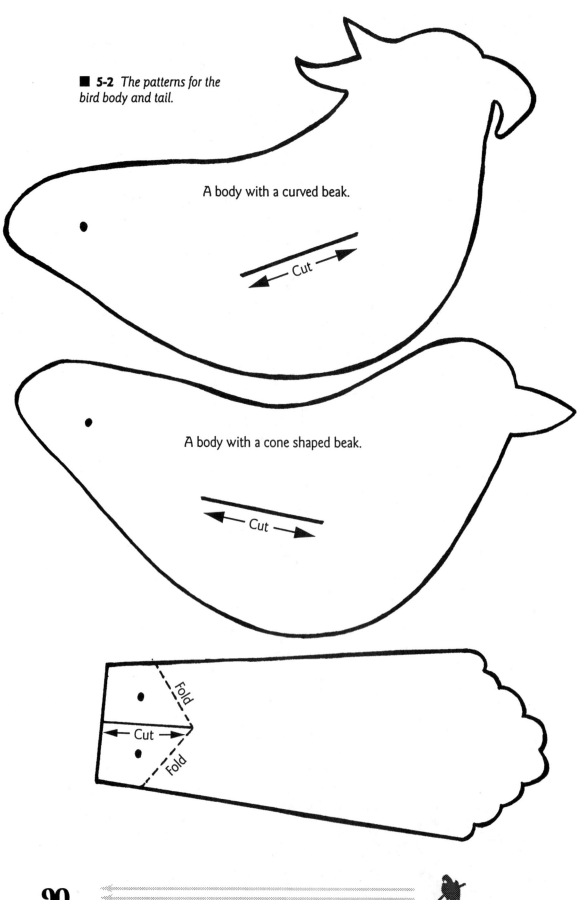

■ **5-2** *The patterns for the bird body and tail.*

A body with a curved beak.

Cut

A body with a cone shaped beak.

Cut

Fold

Cut

Fold

2. Trace and cut out the patterns for the bird body, wings, and tail (Figs. 5-2 and 5-3). Lay the patterns on the paper plate as shown in Fig. 5-4. Draw around the patterns and cut out the bird pieces.

3. Cut a slit in the bird's body as shown on the pattern. Color your bird.

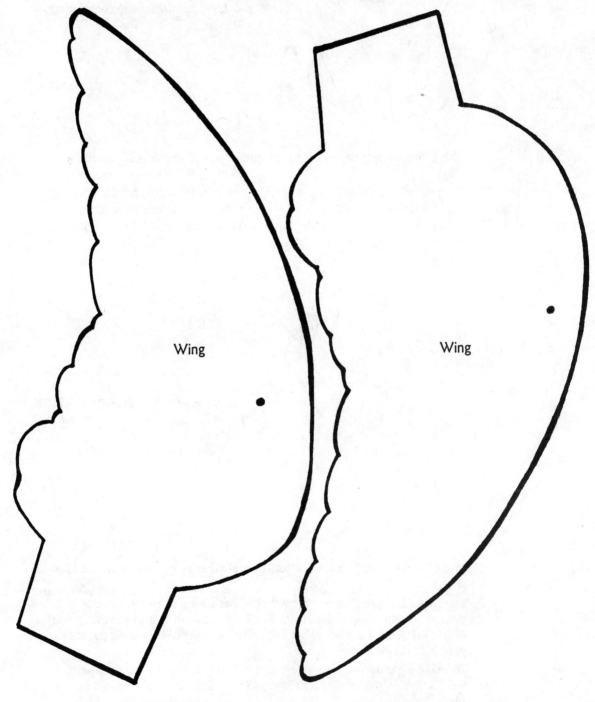

Wing

Wing

■ **5-3** *The patterns for the wings.*

■ **5-4** *Lay the patterns on the paper plate.*

4. A bird folds its feet under his body when flying. Draw feet under its wings.
5. Cut a slit in the tail and fold down the two tabs as shown on the pattern (Fig. 5-5). Slide the tail onto the back of the bird. Make a small hole through both tail tabs and the body, then insert a paper fastener (Fig. 5-6).

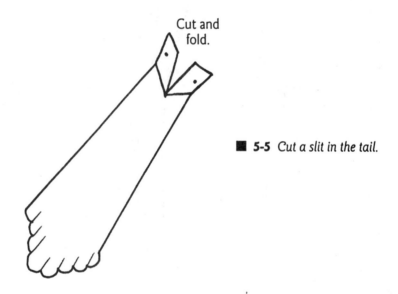

Cut and fold.

■ **5-5** *Cut a slit in the tail.*

6. Insert the two wings in the body slit. Staple them together in the middle (Fig. 5-7).
7. Make a small hole to insert the string in each wing as shown on the pattern. Tie one end of the 20-inch string on one wing and the other end of the string on the other wing. Lift up the middle of the string to make your bird flap its wings.
8. To make a handle for your bird, cut a 1¼-×-11-inch piece of cardboard. Fold it in half. Insert the bird's body in the open end and staple it in place under the wings.

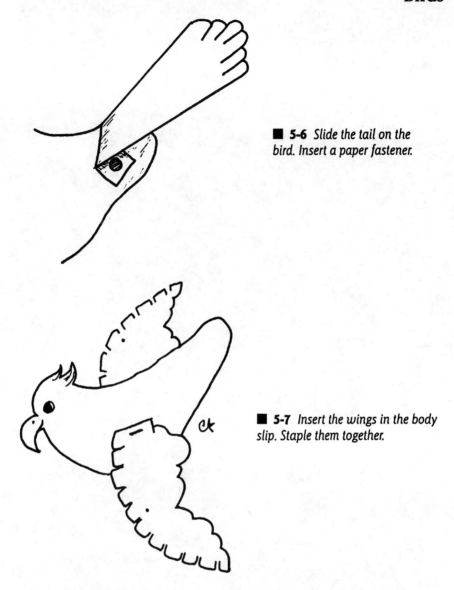

■ **5-6** *Slide the tail on the bird. Insert a paper fastener.*

■ **5-7** *Insert the wings in the body slip. Staple them together.*

9. Write or dictate a report about your bird. What does it need in order to live a happy and healthy life? If your bird were real, what would you do to take care of it?

☞ *Closure*

 Communicating information

Review your initial goals and give the children opportunities to talk about what they have learned. Let them share their favorite parts of the study. Have them discuss ways they can use what they have learned.

Choose one of the following:

1. Let the children write or tape-record a report to go with the type of bird they painted or crafted.

2. Let the children write thank-you letters to the pet shop. Encourage the children to write about their favorite birds and how much they appreciated the visit. The children might want to encourage the pet shop employees to give the birds plenty of attention and love.

chapter **6**

FISH

Science goals

To help children become aware of what these animals are like, how they behave as pets, and how we can take care of them

Teacher/Parent planning

Think about how you can get a fish to the class for a visit. Send a letter home asking parents to bring in a fish for a visit. Perhaps you already have fish in an aquarium in your classroom, or maybe you can take your class to another room where an aquarium is available. Borrow informational books from the library. Prepare to write words about fish on a large sheet of chart paper.

Materials needed for discussion and activities

☐ Live fish for observation
☐ Books from the library
☐ Magnifying glasses

Related words

fish A cold-blooded animal with a backbone, fins, and scales, which lives in water

aquarium A glass or plastic container filled with water as a home for fish and other animals that live in water

gill A body organ that takes oxygen out of water for breathing

oxygen A colorless, tasteless, odorless gaseous element that is a natural part of the earth's atmosphere and is essential for life

tropical Relating to the part of the earth near the equator where the weather is warm and humid

Fish make ideal pets for a classroom or for people who live where they do not have much room to keep a pet. Fish are easy to care for, quiet, and beautiful. You do not have to exercise them because they swim in water throughout the day and night. You can buy fish at a pet store or from someone who has an aquarium with extra fish to sell or give away.

 Visiting with fish

Observing

If you cannot observe fish in the classroom, arrange for the children to see fish by going on a field trip to a pet store. Let the children take magnifying glasses. You might want to read information about fish while you are observing them. You can also label a fish diagram as you watch and read.

If you are able to observe a variety of fish, talk about how each type of fish swims. Some fish dart about the tank while others swim lazily along. Talk about the different sizes and colors of the fish. Do groups of similar fish stay together?

☞ *Making a Fish Diagram*

🔎 *Recording information*

Draw a large diagram of a fish on chart paper (Fig. 6-1). Let the children come up and point to the fish's body parts as you write the words, or let the children label the parts themselves with a magic marker. You might want to label the diagram as you read about each body part.

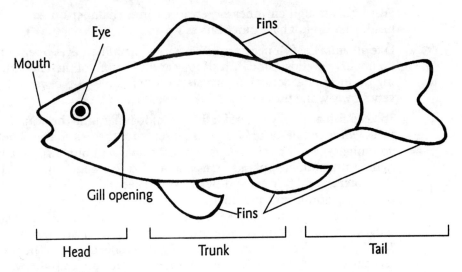

■ **6-1** *A Fish Diagram.*

Fish are animals with backbones so they are called vertebrates. They breathe mainly through gills. They are cold-blooded, which means that their body temperature changes with the temperature of their surroundings. Almost all fish have fins, which they use for swimming. Some kinds of fish begin their lives in eggs. Other kinds are born as very tiny fish. Fish spend all of their lives in water. Like us, fish can see, hear, smell, taste, and feel. Fish continue to grow throughout their lifetime.

Fish have a streamlined body. The head is rounded and blends smoothly into the trunk. A fish has no neck. The trunk connects with the tail. The skin of a fish contains blood vessels and nerves. Most fish have a protective covering of scales.

Fins are movable parts of the fish that help it to swim and keep its balance. A fish moves its fins by using its muscles. Fish swim forward by using side to side movements of the back part of the body, which includes a powerful tail fin. Other fins lie along the back or underside of the fish and steady it in the water. Shoulder and hip fins are used for steering and braking as the fish swims. Fish have a line along each side of their body called a lateral line. This line helps the fish sense the pressure of water around it. The fish can sense fixed or moving objects and can swim without hitting anything.

Fish breathe by getting oxygen from water. Water contains some dissolved oxygen. To get oxygen, fish gulp water through their mouths and pump it over their gills. Their gills absorb oxygen and release carbon dioxide. The water then passes out through the gill openings. If there is not enough oxygen in the water, some fish, such as goldfish, come to the surface and gulp air directly.

Most fish can see to the right and to the left at the same time. Since a fish has no neck, it cannot turn its head. Fish do not have eyelids. Animals that live on land need eyelids to keep their eyes moist and protect them from sunlight. A fish's eyes are kept moist by the water flowing over them.

Fish hear through an inner ear enclosed in a chamber on each side of its head. They do not have outer ears as we do.

Like all animals, fish need rest. Fish "sleep" with their eyes open, since they do not have eyelids. Other fish sleep near the bottom of their aquarium, resting on their side. Some fish just stay in the middle of the water, but move very slowly while they sleep.

To keep fish as pets, you need a fish tank, or aquarium. The aquarium is the fish's world and needs to be a pleasant place for the fish to live. Some things you might see in or on an aquarium are water, a pump, a filter, a heater, a light, a thermometer, plants, gravel, and a lid for the top of the aquarium. The water should be clear and clean. The lid keeps the fish from jumping out of the aquarium and prevents anything from falling into the water. The pump helps to circulate the water and move it through the filter. The filter removes dirt and harmful particles from the water. The heater warms the water. The light provides light, heat, and beauty, especially at night. The thermometer tells you the temperature of the water, so you can keep the water warm enough for the fish. Plants make the tank more attractive, provide shelter and food, and release oxygen into the water. Gravel provides beauty and helps hold plants in place.

☞ *Looking at an aquarium*

Observing
If you are able to observe an aquarium, let the children find and identify the parts of the aquarium.

Let's Create a File Folder Aquarium

Creating a model to learn more about an aquarium and the plants and animals that might live in it; manipulating materials
Use one file folder and two pieces of left over laminating material to create a see-through aquarium (Fig. 6-2). Draw eels, turtles, fish, and water plants with permanent markers. Stand it up for a 3-D effect!

What you need
☐ File folder
☐ Scissors
☐ Two pieces of leftover laminating material (Use the scraps that have already gone through the laminating machine.)
☐ Cellophane tape
☐ Permanent markers in several colors

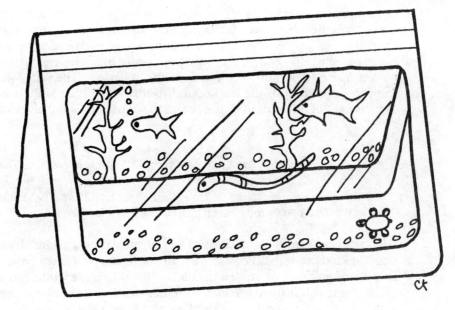

■ **6-2** *The File Folder Aquarium.*

Directions

1. Cut a large rectangular window in each side of the file folder.
2. Tape a piece of laminating material inside the file folder to cover both windows. Your aquarium will look like it's filled with water. Stand it up on a table with the fold at the top.
3. Use permanent markers to draw aquarium plants and animals on both sides of your aquarium.

> *Pet pause* A person who has an aquarium is called an aquarist.

In the wild, fish spend a lot of time looking for food, but as pets they are fed small amounts once or twice a day. The best food for most pet fish is dried food in the form of flakes. A tiny pinch is enough for most fish.

Keeping the water in the tank very clean and healthy is important for the fish. Before water is added, it needs to sit out for two days so that the chlorine, which can harm fish, can disappear. A special solution that causes the chlorine to disappear right away can be bought from the pet store to add to the water. Never use soap to clean the tank. It is harmful to fish.

If an aquarium gets too much light from a window, tiny green plants called algae grow on the sides of the glass and make the water greenish. Then the aquarium will need to be cleaned and moved to where it cannot get so much light.

 Using a siphon

 Manipulating materials; designing investigations
Discuss ways that water can be removed from the aquarium, such as pouring, using a cup, letting it evaporate, and so forth. Remind the children that an

aquarium is usually too heavy to lift. If you can, get a *siphon*, which is a long piece of plastic tubing that carries liquid from one level to a lower level. Fill the siphon with water, then hold your thumbs over each end so no water can come out. Put one end in the aquarium water and one end in an empty bucket. The bucket must be lower than the aquarium. The water will move from the aquarium to the bucket until both sides of the siphon hold the same weight of liquid or until the end in the aquarium is pulled out into the air.

Pet pause *The siphon works because of differences in pressure. The weight of the liquid in the long side of the siphon reduces pressure in the tube. Pressure from the atmosphere on the surface of the liquid forces liquid up the short side (the part in the aquarium) and gravity pulls it down.*

You can choose from many kinds of fish to keep as pets. Goldfish are a very popular kind of pet fish. Pet stores usually have many different types of goldfish. Some goldfish are golden in color, while others are white, blue, red, or black. Some goldfish are speckled with many colors. Goldfish can have large scales, small scales, long fins, short fins, and goggle-shaped eyes.

Pet pause *Goldfish are related to the carp. Goldfish originated in China about 1,000 years ago. They were imported into England in the eighteenth century. They were brought to America by the middle of the nineteenth century.*

Fish are able to float in the water without sinking because they have an internal lifebuoy, called a *swim bladder*, that fills with gas produced by the fish's body.

The common goldfish has a long, arched body, and a wide, short head. It has a forked tail fin. A more fancy breed is called a comet. The comet has larger, more pointed fins. A one-year-old common, or comet, goldfish is about 1 to 2 inches long, not counting its tail. If kept in a very large tank, common goldfish can grow to be 7 or 8 inches long in five years. Goldfish can live to be 20 years old.

Other types of goldfish include fantails, veiltails, moors, orandas, lionheads, shubunkins, telescopes, and celestials.

A goldfish's skin is covered with *scales*. Like tiles on a roof, scales cover a fish's body in regular rows. One part of each scale is beneath the skin, and the other part is free and can be lifted up. Scales are hard and transparent, which means you can see through them. The color of a fish is mainly due to cells that are underneath the scales.

Pet pause *Scales have growth lines that indicate the age of the fish.*

You can keep a goldfish in an aquarium or a large fishbowl. For each goldfish up to 1 inch long you need one gallon of water in the aquarium. Plants are pretty and helpful to the fish. Plants take in waste products, such as carbon dioxide, and use these wastes to grow. Plants give off oxygen, which goldfish need for breathing. The fish also nibble at the leaves and get some food this way. A fishbowl or aquarium should not be kept directly in front of a window.

Goldfish eat just a pinch of food each day. You can buy fish food at a pet store. Be sure not to overfeed your goldfish!

☞ *Testing a goldfish's hearing*

🔍 *Designing investigations*
You can test your goldfish to find out if it hears things. To test it, you need a bell. Feed your fish each day at one corner of the aquarium. Ring the bell as you put in the food. Do not put in any food unless you ring the bell. After about five days, try ringing the bell first. See if your fish rises to be fed just by hearing the sound, then give it some food.

☞ *Researching fish*

🔍 *Finding information*
Gather the children around you as you read informational books. As you read about each type of fish, let the children look for that fish in the books. Let them share what they find. Talk about the many kinds of fish people keep in aquariums.

Let's Create a Comet Goldfish in a Paper Plate Fishbowl

🔍 *Becoming familiar with the anatomy of a comet goldfish by creating a model; manipulating materials; learning to measure with a ruler*
A paper plate can become a fishbowl, and Cream of Wheat cereal can become gravel for your beautiful pet goldfish (Fig. 6-3).

What you need
- ☐ 9-inch white paper plate
- ☐ Scissors
- ☐ Blue construction paper
- ☐ White glue
- ☐ Orange markers
- ☐ Black pen
- ☐ Gold glitter (optional)
- ☐ Ruler
- ☐ Dry grits, Cream of Wheat cereal, or Cream of Rice cereal
- ☐ Liquid food dye (any color)
- ☐ Plastic sandwich bags with twist ties

Directions

1. Fold a sheet of tracing paper in half. Copy and cut out the paper plate fishbowl pattern in Fig. 6-4. Then lay the pattern on the paper plate so the bottom of the bowl is even with the edges of the plates. Draw

■ **6-3** *The Comet Goldfish in a Paper Plate Fish Bowl.*

around the pattern and cut out the bowl. Use the scraps to make the goldfish.

2. Glue the paper plate bottom-side-up on a sheet of blue construction paper so that it looks like a bowl filled with water. Let the glue dry, then trim the paper that is outside the plate, leaving only the "bowl" of "water."

3. Use the pattern in Fig. 6-4 to trace the comet goldfish. Cut it out and color it orange. Add the fins, gills, and eyes with a black pen. If you want to, add glitter. Glue the goldfish in the bowl.

4. To make gravel, pour 1 tablespoon of dry cereal into a plastic sandwich bag. Add three drops of food dye. Close the bag with a twist tie. Shake the bag until the cereal is dyed.

5. Spread glue in the bottom of the bowl. Pour on the dyed cereal. Shake off the excess.

6. To make the bowl stand up, measure and cut a 2½-x-11-inch rectangle out of construction paper, as shown in step 1 of Fig. 6-5. Fold the rectangle in half and glue it to the back of the bowl.

7. Use the ruler to measure a second construction paper rectangle measuring 1 × 6 inches, as shown in step 2 of the illustration. Fold down 2 inches on each end, as shown in step three. Glue it inside the first rectangle to keep it from spreading apart and falling down.

Guppies are very popular pets. Their native home is in the warm, fresh waters of South America. They are peaceful, friendly, and pretty. They are tiny fish,

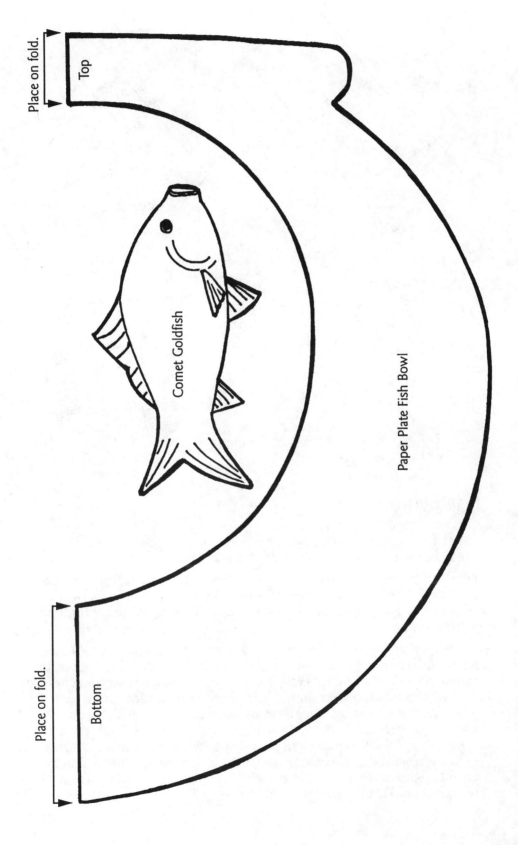

Top

Place on fold.

Comet Goldfish

Paper Plate Fish Bowl

Place on fold.

Bottom

■ **6-4** *The patterns for the Comet Goldfish and the Paper Plate Fish Bowl.*

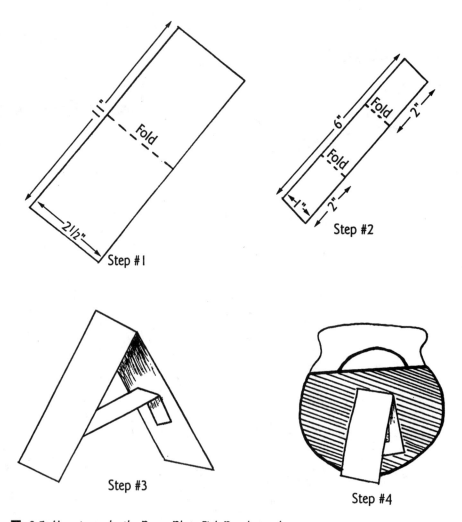

■ **6-5** *How to make the Paper Plate Fish Bowl stand up.*

only 1 to 2 inches long. Guppies are various colors, including orange, blue, white, and yellow. Their tails can have many different shapes.

Angelfish are also very pretty fish. They originally came from South or Central America. Like all tropical fish, they need warm water. They have well-developed lips. Some kinds of angelfish are black lace, golden, blushing, and ghost angelfish.

Tetras are small colorful tropical fish originally from South and Central America. Some types of tetras are splash, cardinal, black, golden, silvertip, lemon, rosy, bleeding heart, flame, and neon tetras. Neon tetras come from the Peruvian Amazon River. In the wild, they live in shaded jungle waters. When they are kept as pets, they need a darkened aquarium with the bottom and sides in dark colors. Black tissue paper can be taped to the sides of the aquarium and floating plants can be added to the water to make the environment as natural as possible. In the neon's natural jungle habitat, rain frequently freshens the water. The aquarist can add boiled rain or tap water weekly to provide the right conditions for the neon tetra.

Natural habitats

 Drawing conclusions; making predictions
"Why is it important for us to know about the natural habitats of animals we acquire as pets? What can happen if we do not provide environments that seem like their natural ones?" (They might die. They might not have babies. They might get sick. They might change in order to adapt to unnatural conditions.)

Let's Create a Shoebox Aquarium

Creating a model to learn more about an aquarium and the plants and animals that might live in it; manipulating materials
Use a shoebox to create an aquarium, then fill it with interesting fish, eels, and underwater plants (Fig. 6-6). Cover the front with plastic wrap for a watery effect! Each child can make his or her own shoebox aquarium, or it can be created as a group project involving three or four children per aquarium.

■ **6-6** *The Shoebox Aquarium.*

What you need
- ☐ Shoebox
- ☐ Scissors
- ☐ Construction paper
- ☐ White glue
- ☐ Markers or crayons
- ☐ Cellophane tape
- ☐ Dental floss for hanging the fish

☐ Dry grits, Cream of Wheat cereal, or Cream of Rice cereal
☐ Liquid food dye (any color)
☐ Plastic sandwich bags with twist ties
☐ Clear plastic wrap

Directions

1. Remove the shoebox lid. Turn the box lengthwise on its side. One side is now the bottom of the box and one side is the top. The open side of the box should be facing you. Inside the box, line the top and sides with light blue paper to resemble water. Line the bottom of the inside with dark or black paper. Glue the paper in place.

2. Use the patterns in Fig. 6-7 to trace fish and water plants onto construction paper. Cut them out and color them. You can also design your own fish and plants to add to your aquarium.

3. Fold down the bottom of each plant and glue it to the bottom of the aquarium.

4. To make gravel, pour 1 tablespoon dry cereal into a plastic sandwich bag. Add three drops of food dye. Close the bag with a twist tie. Shake the bag until the cereal is dyed. Spread glue in the bottom of the aquarium. Pour on the dyed cereal. Gently shake out the excess.

5. Hang up each fish by taping a piece of dental floss to it, and then taping the other end of the floss to the top of the aquarium. If you want to, you can glue the eel in the seaweed.

6. Tape plastic wrap over the front of the shoebox aquarium to make it look like it's filled with water. Cover the outside top and sides of the shoebox with construction paper.

A fish is a living creature that has needs such as food, contentment, and safety. Pet fish need us for survival. They cannot talk to us, so we must watch them carefully and care for them each day. They can add enjoyment to our lives as we observe their beauty and grace and as we discover how they function in a world of water.

☞ Closure

Communicating

Bringing closure to your study is important. Review your initial goals. Give the children opportunities to talk about what they have learned and how they can use this information.

Give each child a fish shape cut from light-colored construction paper. Let each child write a question on one side and the answer on the other side. Let them decorate the side with the question. Put all of the fish in a plastic or glass fishbowl. Sit in a circle and have the fishbowl in the middle. Each child can come up, get a fish, read the question aloud, and call on a volunteer to answer it.

Possible questions and answers might be the following:

☐ What helps a fish breathe? Gills
☐ What helps a fish swim? Fins, tail
☐ What covers a fish's body? Scales

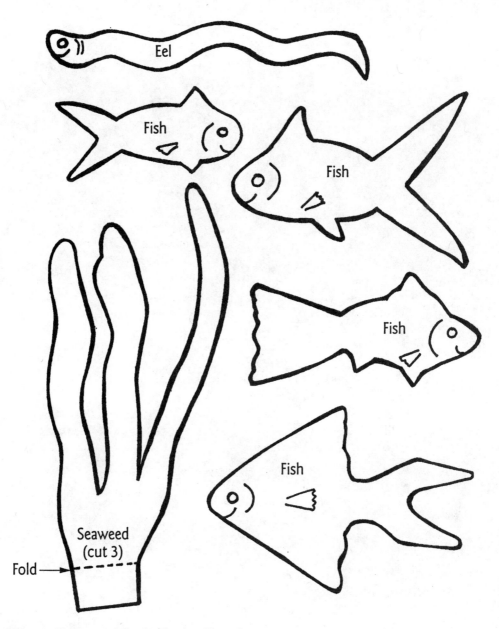

■ **6-7** *The patterns for the Shoebox Aquarium.*

Index

Boldface numbers indicate illustrations

Index

About the Authors

Barbara Dondiego holds a master's degree in education from the University of Virginia, and a bachelor of science degree in foods and nutrition from Oregon State University. She is a state-certified educational consultant who conducts regular workshops for preschool teachers. Barbara is author of TAB's *Crafts for Kids: A Month-by-Month Idea Book, Year-Round Crafts for Kids,* and *After-School Crafts.*

Rhonda Vansant has a doctorate of education from Vanderbilt University, has taught classes at both the elementary and college levels, and serves as an educational consultant. She conducts workshops and gives conference presentations on methodologies for teaching young children. Rhonda is also a member of the National Association for the Education of Young Children and the Association of Childhood Education International.